Legacy of Love

Teaching Future Generations to Care About Animals

By Anna C. Briggs

Co-founder, The National Humane Education Society

With a preface by
William J. Kropp, Executive Director,
The National Humane Education Society

National Humane Education Society

Fostering a sentiment of kindness to animals

Table of Contents

Preface: My Legacy

When I first met the dog who changed my life, I was 13 years old. Today, at age 88, my love for animals continues to grow. I am blessed with a companion named Sheena who keeps me young at heart.

Looking back over these 70+ years, I remember so many animals, so many instances when I was lucky enough to be able to help. Tut, Sport, and Cy were just the first three — there have been literally thousands of cats and dogs, puppies and kittens I have been privileged to know and to love ... and to offer what I could to help them lead happy, healthy lives. My life has been enriched by knowing each and every one of these wonderful creatures.

I am glad that I have been able to make a difference. Of course, the biggest impact came from fulfilling a dream of mine and my husband's to create The National Humane Education Society, dedicated to fostering a sentiment of kindness toward all animals.

When we began The Society, we never even gave a thought to where we would be 50 years later. I could never have predicted that we would be a powerful presence in the animal welfare movement, that we would be more than 400,000 members strong, and that people in every state of the nation would support our work. Their support for animals continues to be truly inspiring!

But while I look back with gratitude on these accomplishments, I know there's still so much to be done for the animals. When I reflect on the days when I was a young girl, I realize we have come a long way. In those days, it was not uncommon to see carriage horses being abused on the streets of major cities. Fortunately, this has stopped.

But although times change, cruelty too often remains. It just gets carried out in a different way. In recent years, a new, cruel "sport" called "horse tripping" has emerged. Horse tripping is practiced in rodeos in the Southwest, where horses are run around an arena and tripped with ropes stretched across the track. When they fall, many are too wounded to be kept alive, so they are killed. Even the ones who remain alive experience excruciating pain and suffering.

And a barbaric practice known as "rendering" threatens not only the lives of animals, but of humans as well. Rendering means feeding ground-up cows and other animals back to other cows. In the human world, this would be known as cannibalism. In England, it has been widely thought that rendering led to the outbreak of mad cow disease.

Whereas the Food and Drug Administration specifically outlaws rendering, numerous loopholes in the regulations make it practicable to use ground animal parts, spray-dried bovine plasma, and whole blood in feed for calves and cows. Farming practices in America include many forms of rendering even today.

So, you see, too often we solve one problem and others appear. That's why our work never ends.

But there's no room for cynicism or inaction. These attitudes only lead to despair. If we care not only about our animals, but also about ourselves, then we must do something now. As Mahatma Gandhi put it, "the greatness of a nation and its moral progress can be measured by the way its animals are treated." It's not how well our economy is going, or how many wars we can win, or whether our influence extends across the globe that ultimately matter it's how we treat one another. And that is mirrored in how we treat the animals in our care. We must show our compassion universally: Until we stop harming all living beings, we are less than fully human.

I wish that I could say that I will leave this earth having fulfilled my lifelong dream of humane treatment for all animals everywhere. Sadly, this is not to be. But, with the help of friends like you, The National Humane Education Society will go forward working to prevent suffering and to stop cruelty long after I'm gone.

I am deeply grateful for all you have done for the animals by supporting our efforts, and I hope this book will help you do even more to help the animals we love.

Introduction: A Belief System in Action

by William J. Kropp
Executive Director
The National Humane Education Society

I became part of The National Humane Education
Society quite by accident. Today, looking back, I think
it was a happy accident, for me and for The Society. I
was able to bring real help to an organization filled with
wonderful people and dedicated to the highest ethical
principles in the treatment of animals. Serving in such a
capacity has been a great joy in my life.

But I'm getting ahead of myself. Let me tell you
exactly how I got involved with the Society.

About 13 years ago, I was introduced to Mrs. Briggs by
her grandson, who is a good friend of mine. In speaking to
me about her work, he stressed that she needed some
management help. Mrs. Briggs and I met several times; as a
result, she asked me to work for The Society as a
consultant. There were two reasons she wanted someone
like me on board:

First, she had become aware of the complexity of life and business. At the time, "The Society" meant mostly "Mrs. Briggs." She was very concerned that, if she were to die suddenly, the organization would not be in a position to continue. Mrs. Briggs asked me to develop a structure and organization for The Society, so it would keep going long after she was gone.

Secondly, she requested that it remain to the extent possible a family organization. She hoped that her children and grandchildren could and would participate, depending on their own interests. She wanted to ensure that her descendants could play an active role in The Society's operation.

I willingly undertook to help Mrs. Briggs. Very early on, however, I discovered that there was no money — that she was supporting The Society with her own meager funds. So instead of organizational design and control, my immediate objective became simply to help The Society survive. I had been scheduled to work 10 hours a week, but this quickly became 30-40 hours a week.

We managed to get through those difficult days. We embarked on a new fund-raising operation, and it began to work. This was the exciting beginning of my tenure at The Society — a real roller-coaster ride!

But I was not unaccustomed to instability. Before working for The Society, I had spent 30 years as a

psychologist, working at a private psychiatric hospital for
children and adolescents. Back in 1966, I was part of a
group of people who set up a group home for children with
epilepsy and emotional disorders; we developed this home
into a clinical treatment program, finally gaining licensure
as a hospital. When I ended my career there, I was the
Director of Admissions and Marketing. Subsequently, I
went back to school and got a Master's degree in Business
Administration.

Shortly afterwards, I met Mrs. Briggs. I worked in
both settings — the home for children and The National
Humane Education Society — for almost 10 years. Then,
as The Society began to grow, I realized that a unique
opportunity was presenting itself. Since The Society
needed someone to direct their fund-raising efforts, and
since the folks here were interested in my staying on, I
decided I could use the change after 30 years of working
with children. On the other hand, I soon learned just how
much similarity there can be between institutional care for
children and the humane care of animals!

Fortunately, things started looking up for The Society
almost immediately. By the end of six or seven months,
The Society's balance sheet was firmly in the black — for
the first time in Society history. I visited Peace Plantation
Animal Sanctuary in Walton (upstate New York) a few
times to determine their needs. Looking at the overall

operations of The Society, I began trying on a limited basis to institute some structural changes.

For a variety of reasons, we concluded that a major focus of The Society for the future should be on educational work. Not only were we already using "education" in our name, we also understood that, in the long run, it would be education rather than hands-on animal care that would bring about social reform. So we developed a tripartite organization, including divisions for humane education, rescue and relief, and direct animal care in a sanctuary setting. While never for a moment abandoning our original intent — to offer Peace Plantation as a sanctuary for stray and abandoned animals and those who were surrendered to us, and never to euthanize healthy animals in the name of population control — The Society's organizational structure, purpose, and reach had grown significantly over the years and required new definition.

From The Society's original 1948 bylaws, we found appropriate language to include in our new mission statement: "To create a sentiment of kindness to animals in children and adults." This key concept has served to guide The Society's development as a service organization. We systematically work to provide the highest standard of care, not only to the animals under our direct care, but also to the many thousands who receive medical attention, care, and shelter with our assistance.

But a non-profit organization like ours can continue this vital work only with a sound financial basis. In essence, I believe that only those non-profit organizations which operate with strong administrative and management policies (essentially as service businesses) will survive in the long run, since the competition for the charitable dollar is just too great. For social change to become a reality — in other words, for everyone to start treating animals with care, love, and dignity — our cause needs to be presented to Americans for decades to come; fiscal soundness can make that possible.

Much of The Society's financial support comes from friends across the nation. To get our message out and to recruit new supporters, The Society mails many letters and information packets each year. Because the image or impression we leave with readers is very important, we are stringent about how we come across in the mail: We combine information on principles of humane care and general humane educational materials with each and every solicitation.

We also publish our *Quarterly Journal,* which always includes a feature article describing a major issue in animal welfare. We write about how the issue — from animal overpopulation to cruel practices in the name of "sport" — developed, The Society's position on it, and what readers can do to help. The Journal is mailed to some 400,000 members every quarter. Through a survey, we learned that, on average, each newsletter is read by four people in addition to The Society member who receives it. That means each issue is read by 1.6 million people — an extremely effective means of getting the word out. We also produce and distribute numerous brochures to educate people nationwide about humane principles.

These are the primary directions we have been taking over the past decade. Within each of our three major program areas, we run eight to ten programs that all foster the same mission. Rather than going off in different directions, we keep expanding our sphere of influence. To give you just one example: Two and a half years ago, we were approached by concerned people in the thoroughbred industry, who asked us to start an equine division — basically, a retirement program for thoroughbred horses who had been racing but who could no longer "pull their weight" financially. We created Greener Pastures, Inc., a fledgling program with 12 animals, and invested significant resources to create a barn, running shed, wells, and other accommodations for these retired racehorses. We anticipate expanding the program to help several thousand horses on farms across the country in the future.

The Society runs an active adoption program out of our Leesburg, Virginia, headquarters. Every six months or

so, about 50 dogs pass through our doors. Having begun
their lives as strays or abandoned creatures, they end up in
loving homes with responsible families. Most are rescued
from shelters, where they had typically been scheduled for
euthanasia. We come in at the eleventh hour. Because the
animals are usually in horrible physical condition, we
provide them with expert veterinary care, get them healthy,
groom them, give them obedience training, and then
advertise for their adoption through local newspaper inserts
every quarter. We have an adoption staff who carefully
interview people interested in adopting an animal. We only
give animals to those who provide the right match and
who will make a lifetime commitment to the animal.

At Peace Plantation, we now have a full-time staff of
24. In addition, we contract with a veterinary practice to
provide all the care necessary at the facility. A veterinarian
in Leesburg handles the animals who come through the
adoption program; similarly, an equine vet in Maryland
handles our horses there.

So, to recap, The Society's current operations include:
- Peace Plantation Animal Sanctuary, serving
  500 animals a day;
- Our adoption services program in Leesburg
  (where, at any given time, we have 30 or so
  animals in our care);
- A spay-neuter program in conjunction with

Peace Plantation Animal Sanctuary, which arranged about 1,200 procedures last year on a no-charge, donation-only basis;

❧ Our educational program, carried out through multi-purpose mailings (including our books, of which this is the fifth), presentations in schools, and community-based educational programs;

❧ Our Enterprise Farm in Cecilton, Maryland, where we are in the planning stages of creating a National Humane Education Center for professionals, paraprofessionals, and animal lovers from all walks of life (similarly, we are involved in the protection of wildlife habitat and open spaces);

❧ Our Greener Pastures equine program; and

❧ Our active search to find and construct another Peace Plantation Animal Sanctuary in the Virginia/West Virginia area — which would entail caring for an additional 700 animals daily! (This will put the number of animals in our direct, daily care at well over 2,000!)

Our overall purpose in sheltering this many animals is to find adoptive homes for all those we can, because their quality of life is so much better with a loving family. However, there will always be some — elderly animals or those with special needs — who won't find an adoptive home; they will be welcome to live out the natural span of their lives with us.

And for the future?

We see our program expanding with the opportunities that will undoubtedly present themselves. We are developing new ways to support The Society, such as an active planned giving program (including wills, bequests, and trusts) and a major donor program focused on annual gifts and pledges. Because we feel that, as an organization, we have to diversify and create new revenue streams, we are involved with several companies in cause-related marketing endeavors.

On the education front, we are rapidly gaining recognition from veterinarians through mutually beneficial collaboration. One of the things we have done educationally is to enable veterinarians to make presentations on topics of interest to folks concerned about animals. The Society markets and sponsors the presentations. In this way, we are continually enhancing and expanding our humane education effort, and it's helping us forge a stronger alliance with the veterinary profession. We have already sponsored eight presentations, and I anticipate we will put on two to three more every month.

We have established an office in Chesapeake City, Maryland, a tourist area with several thousand walk-ins a year, where we can offer our literature and answer particular questions. (It's the precursor to our opening the Humane Education Center in nearby Cecilton.) From there, we organize and administer our educational efforts in the Delmarva area. We have humane educators going into the school systems. In the last six months of 1997 alone, we made presentations to more than 3,000 students.

Our direction for the future is to be professional, well-organized, and well-managed (so that the resources are there to support our good work) and to expand every viable opportunity to carry out our mission.

The book you are holding in your hands is an important part of The Society's overall education efforts. It contains, among other advice and information, 50 tips on promoting better stewardship of the animals with whom we share the earth. We encourage you to pass along the information you gain from reading these pages with friends and relatives. This is an effective way of educating as many people as we can about ethics and the proper care of animals.

But the book also contains a story — the story of The Society's founder and hero: Mrs. Briggs. In her own words, she will tell you about her life, her work, and her strong beliefs. It's a compelling tale with many important lessons for us all.

One of the first questions I ever asked Mrs. Briggs was:
"At any time in New York City alone, there will be 6,000
homeless people on the street. Why should I contribute to
you to take care of a few cats in Walton, New York?" She
said, "Because God's lesser creatures need someone to speak
for them."

As you get to know Mrs. Briggs, you realize she's
probably one of most truly altruistic persons the world has
ever known. Qualities derived from the course of her life ...
her firm, unyielding belief ... and the wisdom that comes
with being 88 years old make her an extremely persuasive
advocate for animals. Mrs. Briggs has always been a
woman of modest means who cares little about money.
The only time money becomes an issue is when someone
needs something and she doesn't have it to give — then she
is profoundly bothered. I think of her, in all seriousness, as
the "Mother Teresa" of animals.

It has been my great privilege to help Mrs. Briggs to
accomplish her mission. As I see it, the great challenge for
The Society is to thoroughly incorporate Mrs. Briggs' belief
system into our day-to-day operations, so that we can
carry on in her spirit when she is no longer with us.
Preserving her values about life and the basic rights of
animals is the best way we know to celebrate her life and
provide meaning and support to future generations of
animal lovers. This is what I mean when I say The Society

is a "belief system in action."

I have a great concern for ethics and social reform. I believe that, over the course of time, the fight for animal rights has mirrored problems in our society. When we work on our attitudes and practices toward animals, we also improve the kind of society we live in. I'll leave you with two quotations that I think sum it up — and express Mrs. Briggs' philosophy as well:

"Non-violence leads to the highest ethics, which is the goal of all evolution. Until we stop harming all other living beings, we are still savages."
— *Thomas A. Edison (1847-1931)*

"The day will come when men such as I will look upon the murder of animals the way we now look upon the murder of men."
— *Leonardo da Vinci (1452-1519)*

CHAPTER 1:
One Bright Spot in My Life

Often, when my work on behalf of animals has thrown a spotlight in my direction, I have been asked why. . . why I came to love animals so very much, and why I have devoted most of my life to doing what I could to help them. I can never answer these questions easily, because the answer seems so obvious to me: Because I love animals, I cannot stand idly by while they suffer.

But there's more to it than that. I think I have a special understanding of how animals feel when they are lost, abandoned, or neglected. For — while I was never really mistreated — I knew abandonment, loneliness, and despair as a child. Though my life since then has contained much joy, I don't think I shall ever forget the sadness of my childhood. And I know I will always want to do whatever I can to prevent others from experiencing those emotions.

Please do not think that I was not loved, or that anyone was cruel to me. Far from it — but circumstances beyond anyone's control overwhelmed our family early on. My father died when I was three, leaving my mother with four children to support on her meager wages from a Government job. She struggled to keep the family together, but finally she took the advice of relatives and placed us in orphanages.

My sister, Margaret, and I were sent to St. Vincent's Orphanage in Washington, D.C., our home town, and my two brothers were sent to St. Joseph's Orphanage. But though we were just a few miles from home, we were petrified with fear. The terror I felt on my first night there is still clear in my mind these many years later. Looking around, we saw a huge building with many corridors and 150 girls of all ages. It was confusing, strange, and — that first night — an unfriendly place.

Like many a lost puppy or homesick kitten, all we wanted in the world was to go home to Mother. But we could not. And when the Sisters put Margaret in a separate dormitory for older girls, I screamed so loud and so long that the Sister in charge finally had to allow my sister to come and keep me company for the night. It was the only way anyone could hope to get some sleep!

Young people today might wonder what it was like to live in an orphanage. In St. Vincent's, the orphan's life was not a bad one. Regimented, yes: Bells rang and we formed lines; obedience was firmly demanded. We had to make our own beds and perform various duties. We kept the corridors waxed and shining, every piece of furniture dusted, and all the clothes mended. It was hard work; still, we thrived. The food we ate, though bland, was nourishing and wholesome. And even though we missed our family members and our home, the Sisters were good to us.

But I can remember the days when the halls were full of whispers that someone was coming to look us over for possible adoption. I did not realize that Margaret and I were not eligible, since we still had our mother. The prospective adoptive parent would arrive, and we would all be lined up in the playroom.

I'm sure each girl hoped fervently, as I did, that she would be chosen! In our lonely children's hearts, the hope of a real home still lived on. . . the hope of our own loving family. But I was never chosen. Each time I was passed over, I was despondent.

I wonder if this is how dogs and cats feel, penned up in small cages in animal shelters, longing for their home, watching a friendly human being walk by, hoping without words for the love every animal thrives on.

At least we human orphans were not threatened with impending death when we were not chosen for adoption!

But however lonely I might have felt at the orphanage, I was soon to know an even less pleasant reality. After Margaret and I had spent several years at St. Vincent's, Mother decided to bring Margaret home. For some reason, she sent me to live with an aunt and uncle in Frederick, Maryland. The separation from my sister puzzled and hurt me. But in those days you did not question your parents; you did as you were told. I had no choice: Off to Frederick, Maryland I went.

There I was enlisted to do all the chores for the

household. In those days, there were few modern
conveniences, so housework was long and laborious.
Having been well trained at the orphanage, I took up my
tasks without hesitation. There was not a moment of time
to spare for playing at home. Worse yet, I was told that I
could not even play at recess at school. . . because my aunt
forbade me to get my dress dirty!

Soon I was given additional duties: I became
responsible for the entire family's laundry. Remember,
there were no washing machines or dryers in those days, no
drip-dry clothes, nothing to make the task quicker or easier.
I knew many a tired and discouraged moment before the
age of 12, leaning over a washboard, feeling very alone.

In the summer, my aunt — like most country people of
that era — did an enormous amount of canning. So I spent
my summer days washing Mason jars and preparing fruits
and vegetables. Bushels and bushels of beans, tomatoes,
peas, squash, peaches, and apples passed through my young
fingers. And then there were the jellies and preserves!

For the four years I lived at my aunt's, I could not even
enjoy the simple pleasure of reading. Though her stepson
had a few interesting-looking books in the bookshelf —
including some Horatio Alger volumes — I was told to read
only the Bible or Pilgrim's Progress. Before this edict was
handed down, I had a chance to read one of the Alger
books. Then I was told that such books were not suitable
reading for girls, and I was forbidden to touch them.

But the rags-to-riches, action-filled Alger stories were

tempting to a curious child. Taking pity on me, one of my friends at school brought me an Alger book to read there. But one day the teacher caught me reading it, instead of my textbook. I was soundly scolded. Worse yet, Miss Rinehart reported my crime to my aunt the next Sunday morning after church. My aunt glared at me as only she could, and I burst into tears.

I was lucky that day, however. Our pastor, Mr. Royal, overheard my outburst and asked me what was wrong. I was crying too hard to speak, so my aunt explained my grievous misbehavior. To his everlasting credit, Mr. Royal defended me.

"I should think Miss Rinehart could do better things at church than tattle on a little girl who wasn't doing any harm," he said firmly. My aunt never gave me the punishment I'm sure I would have received had not Mr. Royal — the father of two young girls himself — intervened.

Truly, there is no end to the fantasies an unhappy child can create! From that day forward, I dreamed that Mr. Royal was my father, and that his daughters were my sisters. I got through my gruelling household chores by pretending I was doing them for my own family, the Royal family.

These were the darkest days of my childhood. I longed for my mother and sister. I longed for play, and for playmates. My aunt forbade me even to play with dogs. She said she had been mauled as a child. Therefore, she said

I must cross the street if I saw one. Not knowing dogs, I had no choice but to obey.

When I think today of the many thousands of wonderful dogs who have given me joy, I only wish I could have had a dog friend in those sad, lonely years.

Those years with my aunt stand out in memory as years of isolation and yearning, hard work and little reward for a child so young. I am sure my aunt never meant to mistreat me, but she certainly saw my role more as servant than as family member.

Try as she might, however, my aunt could not suppress all the joy in my life. She kept a canary in a cage in her parlor. The beautiful bird sang and chirped happily, keeping me company on my household rounds. When my aunt took her nap, I stole the time to talk to him for a few moments. I loved taking care of him — cleaning his cage, feeding him, and fixing his bath.

As has been true so many times in my life, in those years an animal gave me the gifts of love, pleasure, and companionship. That little canary was the one bright spot in my life — a spirit-restoring presence in a sad little girl's days.

Today, when I have an opportunity to do something for an animal, I think of that canary, and I'm grateful to be able to return the favor.

I only wish more animals were free to share their sweet companionship in good health and good spirits, as God so clearly intended them to do!

CHAPTER 2:
Tut, Sport, and a Man Called Briggsie

I f you, dear reader, are an animal-lover as I am, you will understand why I am so determined to spare animals unnecessary pain. And you will also understand why I sometimes say my life really began only after I returned from my aunt's home in Frederick, Maryland, and I began to get to know some animals first-hand.

Though I did not like to complain, I reached a turning point just after my thirteenth birthday, in early December of 1923. I wrote to Mother asking her to send me the train fare to come home for Christmas. I asked her, too, if there was any way I could return home permanently. I was so unhappy, so lonely, and yet I had never had an opportunity to tell Mother this when she visited me in Frederick. Somehow she scraped together the train fare, and I had my chance at last.

I will never forget stepping off the train at Washington's Union Station and into the arms of my sister, Margaret, and my brother, Jack. How happy I was to see them! At last, I felt free — for the first time in my life. The three of us celebrated with a chocolate sundae, bought at a delicatessen on Wisconsin Avenue. It was my first chocolate sundae ever, a wonderful treat made even more delicious by the joy of being with my brother and sister.

My family was living in a tiny, four-room house in Georgetown, now a very fancy neighborhood, but then just a working-class, down-to-earth place. My coming home meant that Margaret and Mother would have to share their bedroom with me. I was grateful that they seemed to do so willingly. Now I had to adjust to having no electricity and no central heating, luxuries I had known at the orphanage and at my aunt's house. But these were small deprivations in my mind. At last I was home!

Best of all, though, at last I got to know a dog — a five-week-old puppy named Tut, given to my sister, Margaret. Because Margaret worked as an addressograph operator, it was my job to care for Tut before and after school. A world of pure joy opened up to me! The puppy and I spent every available moment together. Caring for Tut was not a chore to me, but an endless delight.

When I looked into Tut's warm brown eyes, when I played with her, when I stroked her smooth, warm coat, I could only think how very, very wrong my aunt had been about dogs!

But this paradise could not last. Six months after we got Tut, my mother decided she could not let me keep her because she was a female. I had no idea what the implications of being female were, and why that would mean that Tut would have to go — but once again, there was no arguing with one's mother in those days. At the time, neither Mother nor I knew about spaying. To

Mother, there was no alternative, but I was crushed at the idea of having to give Tut away.

I asked every friend and acquaintance if they could take Tut, but no one could. I decided to take her to the delicatessen where I had enjoyed my first ice cream sundae. There I stood on the street with Tut in my arms, asking passersby if they could give my dog a home. It took everything in me to offer Tut over to other people — people I didn't even know! But it had to be done.

At last, two young men approached me. Seeing the tears stream down my face, one of them offered to take Tut. He said she could live at his office where he sold coal. I watched Tut to see how she reacted to him. They took to each other, and thus I lost my first real friend.

Heartbroken, I went home. I was devastated at the loss of Tut. Somehow, a few days later, I managed to get a nickel and I called the man who had taken her. He said she was doing fine. After that I thought it best not to call him any more.

More changes were coming. Mother had her eye on a house for sale in northeast Washington, on Capitol Hill, and she had managed to work overtime long enough to scrape together a deposit. In February 1924, we moved. Still grieving for Tut, now I had to adjust to a new school and classmates. Fortunately, Valentine's Day was just around the corner, and when Valentines were distributed, I received some from my new schoolmates. I felt much better. That was a good school year for me, with an

interesting teacher and nice new friends, and gradually I
recovered from the loss of Tut.

As I got to know my new neighborhood, I met many
people who were out walking their dogs. One lady told me
about the Animal Rescue League not too far from my new
home. I thought to myself, "It must be a wonderful place if
they have dogs!" I asked her for directions. The next
Sunday afternoon, I ran most of the way there.

Leona, the lady in charge, took me to the kennels. I
had never seen a kennel before. Leona told me that not
every dog would find a home. I determined that I would at
least give them some extra love and caring, and every
Sunday after that I ran down Capitol Hill to the Animal
Rescue League, where Leona let me feed, water, and play
with the dogs. My life was immeasurably happier now!

I would run back home after my hours at the League,
overflowing with stories about the dogs I loved so much. I
was overjoyed when Mother said I could have a male terrier
puppy if the League had one to give me. She believed a
terrier would kill any rats that might threaten our
household. I myself did not care what kind of dog we got.
Any dog would be wonderful!

When I went to the League on Palm Sunday 1924,
Leona told me she had a puppy for me. He was curled up
in a cage, sound asleep, a wee little pup of just six weeks, all
white except for a bit of tan on his ears. Leona handed him
to me with a big smile. I was ecstatically happy. I
managed to thank her and took my precious ball of fur to

show Mother. I named him "Sport," and with his presence in my life, the pain remaining from Tut's loss truly began to fade from my heart and mind.

I no longer had time to grieve over Tut, since Sport demanded a lot of care. He was very good at night, but as the sun rose, he would whimper — lonely for his mother and his littermates, no doubt. I would race downstairs and hold him until Mother got up at 6 a.m. Then I fed Sport and took him for a walk, taking tiny short steps so as not to hurry him. When I left for school, he settled down for a nap. I raced home during lunch time to feed him and take him out for his constitutional. He slept again in the afternoon, and after school he stayed in the yard until after the evening meal. We fed Sport table scraps. It didn't take much to fill him up since he was so tiny.

As Sport grew, it became clear that he was not going to kill rats as Mother had hoped. One day, I fed Sport outside, then watched him let a rat come right up and eat his food. Wisely, I thought, Sport had decided to give the rat plenty of room! Rats were not his enemies. He might have even thought of them as friends! I decided to feed Sport inside the house only from then on, but the rats kept coming, as if they expected something. I fed them leftover bread. To me, they were animals like any others. But you can imagine how Mother felt when she found out! She promptly put a stop to my rat-feeding.

Soon Mother decided Sport was not fulfilling his duties as expected. Now a medium-sized dog, Sport obviously had no intention of killing anything. The handwriting was on the wall: Sport was going to have to go. When Mother handed down this decision, I wanted to run away with my dog, but my common sense prevailed. I went to Leona at the Animal Rescue League.

"Sport will have to be put to sleep if you bring him here," she told me. There was no way I was going to let that happen to my happy, healthy friend! So I went to see the lady who had first told me about the League.

"You know, I've heard about a farm for homeless animals," she said. "It's run by a Mr. Briggs. Why don't you telephone him?" She looked up his phone number for me. I called, my hopes high for my little dog. The lady who answered the phone said she would give Mr. Briggs my message, but he never called me.

On a very cold January day in 1925, I was talking with a neighbor in front of my house when a large collie came up to me. Icicles were clinging to the fur of this beautiful, obviously purebred dog; he bore no identification. The neighbor had never seen him before, nor had I. As we pondered what to do, a middle- aged man stopped and asked us if the dog was lost.

"I don't know, but I think so," I told him, "and we don't know what to do about him."

The kindness in the man's blue eyes was readily apparent. "I run a farm for homeless animals," he said. "I can send a man tomorrow to pick up the dog, if we can find shelter for him tonight."

I looked at him in astonishment. "You must be Mr. Briggs!" I exclaimed.

Indeed, it was Mr. Briggs. Already I thought he seemed like the kindest man I had ever met.

"I called your house weeks ago," I told him, "and I left you a message, and you never called back!"

It turned out that the lady who took my message was his cousin. She had a habit of not passing on messages about animals in distress, because she didn't want Mr. Briggs to bring them to the house, even though it was not her home. Now that he knew my story, Mr. Briggs would be able to help me. I was so relieved!

I took the collie home to try to keep him in our garage overnight, so Mr. Briggs could have him picked up the next day. But when the man came for the dog, the collie had managed to find a way out of the enclosure, and was gone. I explained to the driver that, though there was no collie to pick up, I had to give up my own dog, Sport, and asked him to take my pet to Mr. Briggs' farm.

When the man picked up my Sport to put him into the truck, I ran into the house to cry my eyes out. But at least I knew he would not have to be put to death.

Months went by. I wondered about Sport, about how he was doing. Once again I spent my days grieving for a dog I loved and had been forced to give up.

Eventually, I met Mr. Briggs on the street when he was out walking his own dog. I asked him about Sport, but he did not know specifically about my dog. He invited me to

join a party of other ladies who visited the farm on
Sundays, if my mother would give me permission. My
heart leapt with joy when Mother said yes, and a trip was
arranged for the next Sunday.

When we arrived at the farm, located in what was
then the Maryland countryside, I jumped out of the car,
wildly excited about the prospect of seeing my Sportie
again. I "met" every one of the 150 dogs at the farm, but
Sport was not there. The lady in charge told me that a
white terrier with tan ears had been adopted by a family
with two children a few months before. My heart sank
because I would never see Sport again, but I was happy for
my little dog. He was in good hands, and I knew it would
be selfish to wish to have him back again.

That day, Mr. Briggs showed me around his 80-acre "Be
Kind to Animals Rest Farm." In addition to the 150 dogs,
there were 65 cats, 10 horses, and a good many cattle. I
held some of the dogs while Mr. Briggs treated them for
mange. Though he worked hard as an attorney during the
week, Mr. Briggs loved animals so much that he devoted
every spare moment to their rescue and care. I had never
met anyone so generous with his love and caring before. I
left the Farm with a new sense of joy in my heart. Just
knowing about the Farm, and about Mr. Briggs, made me
deeply happy.

My visits to the Farm became a regular occurrence. I
lived for each Sunday to arrive. In 1925, I got my driver's
license — a rather rare thing for a young woman in those

days — and I became the regular Sunday driver of the
Humane Education Society's new vehicle, a Model A
sedan, almost luxurious with its heater and automatic
windshield wiper.

Every Sunday, I was getting to know James P. Briggs
better and better. And every Sunday, I found there was
more and more to admire.

Mr. Briggs had started his organization in 1920,
mortgaging his home to purchase the 80-acre property that
became the "Be Kind To Animals Rest Farm." He built the
Farm's animal pens mostly by himself, learning carpentry
as he went along.

In addition to rescuing animals and taking them to the
Farm, Mr. Briggs held public meetings to inform people
about the suffering of animals in steel-jaw traps,
laboratories, cruel sports and practices, roadside zoos, and
farms and slaughterhouses. He struggled tirelessly to
publicize the plight of animals, writing letter after letter to
William Randolph Hearst, Sr., trying to get the great
publisher interested in exposing the cruelty in laboratories.
I helped him with this correspondence, typing some of the
letters. We were so gratified when Mr. Hearst devoted the
centerfold of The American Weekly to this important
subject.

Though I had been forced to drop out of school and
take a job at a dry cleaner's to help my family's finances, I
was learning a lot about humane work from Mr. Briggs in
those teenage years. In fact, I was forming my vocation

with his help. He taught me how to get people involved, how to care for animals, how to launch an effective protest against inhumane practices. He inspired me, nurturing my childlike love for animals into an adult commitment, encouraging me to be a vegetarian, as he was.

Until then I had never heard of a vegetarian, but in practice, I had just about become one. When Sport had been with us, I realized he needed meat in addition to the table scraps we gave him. I was only too glad to give him my share, along with a lot of gravy I would make and pour over any leftovers we might have had. Nobody had ever heard of canned dog food in those days!

For Mr. Briggs, being a vegetarian followed out of his commitment to animals. He told how cattle and sheep on trains and in slaughterhouses suffered miserably. From that day on, I have never eaten flesh, and I have never missed it. Nor did my children eat meat or fish. Yet, contrary to popular belief, we were all healthy, able to out-work many of our meat-eating counterparts!

With Mr. Briggs' help, I learned how to rescue and care for animals who had been terribly mistreated, and soon I had an opportunity to test my skills on my own. In the spring of 1925, a friend told me about a next-door neighbor who was beating his German Shepherd almost daily. Apparently the man wanted the dog to act like Rin-Tin-Tin, then a popular canine matinee idol. But no amount of training, shouting, and beating made the poor dog do tricks like the man had seen on the movie screen. Though the

man had named the dog "Cy" — short for "Cyclone" —
there was nothing energetic about this oft-beaten, pathetic
animal.

My friend told the man about me, and that I would be
willing to take Cy off his hands, but the man would not
relent. The poor dog was in terrible shape, afraid even to
walk. This infuriated the man even more, and he whipped
him mercilessly. Finally the man realized he would never
win this battle with Cy, and that no one would buy him in
the shape he was in. So he called my friend and said, "You
tell that friend of yours she had better come and get this
dog before I kill it."

When my friend called, I ran to the man's house
immediately. Thinking I might hurt him, the dog shook
and looked for a hiding place. My heart went out to the
poor thin creature, and though he was nearly full-grown, I
picked Cy up and carried him home.

When I put him on the floor, he ran behind a chair and
put his head under it, trying to find shelter.

Of course I knew Mother would likely be very
unhappy about Cy's presence in our home. But she, too,
admired Rin-Tin-Tin, and because Cy was a German
Shepherd, I thought she might give him a chance. I knew I
could fall back on Mr. Briggs if Mother would not relent.
To my surprise, however, Mother felt sorry for Cy, even
though it was obvious he was in no shape to catch any
rats!

It took months to restore Cy to health, months of

tender loving care I was only too glad to give. I would speak soothingly to him, kneeling on the floor if he was hiding. For a long time, Cy would not come out of his hiding place unless I coaxed him. Eventually, he would come out for my sister, but my brothers apparently reminded him forcefully of his former owner, and he stayed away from them. It took several months before Cy would accept their overtures.

By summertime, I could take Cy into the front yard, holding him and stroking him. He needed the support of my touch and constant "baby talk" in order to believe that all was well.

He held his tail between his legs so much that people thought it had been cut off, so I taught him how to wag his tail again, moving it gently with my hand for five minutes at a time. Eventually he started wagging it himself, and the day came when he no longer kept it hidden between his legs. How happy that made me!

Though he still liked to hide behind his chair, Cy gradually grew bolder, happily running in the park with me. And one day, with the help of some puppies, he learned to trust Mother.

Someone had asked me to keep a couple of puppies for a few hours, which I did gladly. When Mother returned from work, and I explained that the puppies were not permanent additions to the household, she knelt down to play with them. Cy was very interested and watched Mother avidly as she petted the little puppies. Inching forward, Cy came over to investigate. Seeing that she liked the puppies, Cy realized that she might like him, too! Suddenly, the ice was broken. Mother reached down and patted Cy on the head, and Cy actually wagged his tail happily. I was thrilled!

After that day, Cy never had the shakes again. But still he had never barked. One day, though, we were both on the third floor of the house. Someone was at the door, and Cy ran downstairs barking. I followed him, delighted, and threw open the door. I shouted to the unsuspecting bread man, "My dog barked! Isn't that great?" I'm sure the man thought I was a lunatic. After all, what would you expect of a full-grown German Shepherd?

I explained Cy's story, and the bread man told me that until that day he had never known we even had a dog. Cy now had the confidence to be a watch dog! I was thrilled, and even Mother was pleased: At last, a dog who could pull his weight in our household!

Cy was smart, too. Though I never tried to teach him any tricks, Cy learned to run and get his leash whenever I combed my hair in front of the mantelpiece mirror. When we went to the store, he seemed to want to carry something home, so I gave him a small basket. He would carry a lightweight item in it as we walked home together companionably. In fact, Cy became a real expert on grocery-buying. When he knew I was about to go out, he would carry Mother's purse to her by the strap. She would take out a five- or ten-dollar bill, which Cy would carry to me. Then he would pick up his little basket, ready to go to the store.

On our walks, Cy and I often encountered Mr. Briggs, out walking his dog. Sometimes we would sit together, and Mr. Briggs would confide in me about his struggles to keep the farm going. Getting adequate help was a constant concern; caretakers did not want to stay at a place without central heating, electricity, or running water. I felt so sorry for this dedicated man who worked all day in the city, then spent every available moment — and every available dollar — to care for the animals he loved.

Though there were many years between us, Mr. Briggs and I seemed to have a special understanding. Certainly we had a shared commitment to helping animals, but Mr. Briggs was equally kind to people — especially to me, I thought. Whenever he thought of a special pleasure I might like, he saw to it that I had the opportunity to enjoy it, by giving me tickets to a movie about animals, for example. My admiration for Mr. Briggs was growing into real love, and one day I let my feeling show.

We were out walking our dogs when I thought of something I had wanted to tell him. Without thinking, I blurted out, "Oh, Briggsie," the special name I called him in my mind. Embarrassed, I told him I had never intended to call him that, but he laughed and said he was glad of it.

Briggsie began to meet me almost every evening, after my shift at the dry cleaner's ended at 8:00. Though I was only 17 when he asked me to marry him, I had no doubts.

I knew my family and friends would disapprove of our age difference, but we both knew in our hearts that it could be bridged — and that it already had been.

On my 18th birthday, December 9, 1927, Briggsie and I went to Ellicott City, Maryland, where we were married in a parsonage. When the ceremony was over, the pastor told us he never married anyone unless he felt they were right for one another. He confided that he was absolutely certain that we would make a good married life together.

And that we did. For the next 18 years, I knew the great happiness of being married to the kindest man I have ever met — a man who would do anything to help people or animals in need.

Today I like to think that, through our love, Briggsie and I were able to help the innocent creatures he loved so much. And it is in his memory that I continue the work we started together — work I will do with love in my heart until I am no longer able to continue it.

CHAPTER 3:
A Refuge and a Haven: Peace Plantation

For the 18 years of my marriage to Briggsie, I knew what it meant to be truly in love. To me, the man was an angel — a loving husband, a gentle father, a tireless worker for the innocent animals who could not help themselves.

Once married, we moved to the Be Kind to Animals Rest Farm, living in part of the caretaker's house. I got used to kerosene heaters, oil lamps, and an oil cookstove once again. Now, too, I learned to carry water long distances, in buckets, uphill when our rusty old pump broke down, as it often did. People think of these things as hardships, and perhaps I would, too, if I had to do them again today, but at that time they did not seem so difficult, because we shared all the work.

My life was happy and busy. I drove Briggsie to work in Washington six days a week. Three times a week, I went to a bakery to buy two-day-old bread for our animals, and then on to an abattoir (a slaughterhouse) to get the cheapest available meats, beef lungs, and livers. I hated going there, hearing the animals being driven to their slaughter, but I had no choice: our animals had to eat.

Then I'd go back to the farm and help prepare the food

for 200 dogs and 70 cats. Fortunately, we could feed the larger animals, horses and cattle, on the hay and grain the farm produced. Then, when the animals had all been fed for the day, I'd drive back to Washington and pick up my husband. Often, on the return trip, we'd stop to pick up an animal to take back to the farm with us.

After his workday was done, Briggsie spent long hours taking care of the animals and repairing kennels. In fact, this was the pattern for the rest of his life: Work all day at a demanding office job, then work at night and on the weekends in his efforts to help animals. In spite of this exhausting routine, I never heard my husband say "I'm tired." Though in later years he became a bit stooped from leaning over his desk for so many hours, his abundant love for life never abated.

The Briggs Family Grows

When people ask me today how I keep going in spite of discouragements, I tell them I learned my optimism from Briggsie. I don't believe he knew how to get really discouraged — though he had some hard blows, especially when we lost the Be Kind to Animals Rest Farm.

With the arrival of our first child in March 1929, we had been forced to move to more congenial living quarters in the city with running water and electricity, but we managed to keep the Farm, hiring a babysitter to watch our son Jim while I took these trips. Times were hard. Often we found ourselves having to beg or borrow money in order to feed the animals at the Farm. How I hated pleading for money! I had no choice, with so many mouths to feed, but I detested it nonetheless.

We tried many avenues to make some extra income, including opening a candy store. I learned to make candy and worked hard, long hours turning out all sorts of delectable items, but still we found it hard to come out ahead.

Though we continued the candy business, hoping that it might turn a real though modest profit someday, things only got worse for us financially. Of course, there was still much joy in our lives: Our son Bobby was born in April 1931, and we continued our work with the animals, though under increasingly difficult conditions. But in 1932, the economic disaster known as the Depression finally robbed us of our farm. For want of $6,500, we lost it. And though I was not too proud to beg on behalf of my animals, there was no way to raise this enormous sum of money in those bleak days.

We were heartbroken, but there was nothing we could do other than try our best to find homes for the animals then at the farm. With the help of Mrs. Kibbie of Bide-A-Wee, a humane organization in New York which took in 150 of our least-likely-to-be-adopted dogs, we placed every animal in a good home.

And so it was that the doors closed on the Be Kind to Animals Rest Farm. Briggsie turned his attention to the needs of animals in laboratories and steel traps. As for me, I closed the candy store in 1933, choosing to find a job with a regular income. But first, with Briggsie's encouragement, I decided to return to high school and get my diploma, which I received in 1936. Fortunately, a kind, loving, and dependable woman named Ruby Brown had come into our lives; Ruby helped with our children while I attended classes. She was a great blessing to our growing family, especially when son, Jack, was born in 1924 and daughter, Virginia, in 1937.

I named my daughter Virginia after my friend Virginia Sargent, President of the Animal Protective Association, who ran an animal shelter. I helped Miss Sargent whenever I could in the kennels; she in turn allowed me to board animals in need at her facility until good homes could be found for them. Thanks to Miss Sargent, I was able to continue the animal rescue work Briggsie and I had been so devoted to at the farm. During these years I also worked with a lady named Alice Morgan Wright. We who loved animals formed a network all around the area, doing whatever we could to help animals. Both Miss Sargent and Miss Wright were instrumental in my work and to The National Humane Education Society as it exists today.

These were busy years, with my young family, my animal rescue work, and, as of April 1941, a secretarial job with the U.S. Army. Since Briggsie was so much older than me, I realized that I needed to prepare myself to support my children. The last thing I wanted was to be unable to

keep my family together if my husband died — the same
thing that had happened to my mother, splitting our family
apart. Since Briggsie's health was not good, I urged him to
retire. But this hard-working family man would not hear
of it.

On December 7, 1941, as the Pearl Harbor attack was
announced over the radio, Briggsie and I were signing
papers to buy a house in Riverdale, Maryland. We moved
our family there, and from then on both of us worked six
days a week, and, because of the war, often on Sundays,
too.

Despite our long, hard hours and our concerns for our
nation and its allies, our family was thriving during those
war years. Jim, our oldest son, had excelled in school. He
graduated from high school in 1945, at the age of 15, and
was accepted early by the Georgetown University School of
Foreign Service. That summer was a good one for our
children, who loved living in Riverdale and had many
friends.

Briggsie was working harder than ever to spare dogs
from vivisection, pushing for the passage of the Dog
Exemption Bill by Congress. On September 8, 1945, he
traveled to Philadelphia to talk with colleagues there about
the proposed legislation. I picked him up upon his return at
Union Station, noticing how very tired he looked and how
slowly he walked toward the car. He did not say much and
I did not press him for details of his visit.

We had gone only a few blocks when he asked me to

stop for a bit. I saw that he was in pain. I wanted to take him to the doctor, but he said no. I soon realized that he was going into a coma. I rushed him to a hospital, but the shot of adrenalin he was given did not revive him.

Jim and Jack were with me. I hugged my sons as I broke the news of their father's death. Then we went home to tell Bob and Virginia, or Ginger, as she is now called. My children had never known death before. They had never even been to a funeral! The boys tried not to burden me with their sorrows, spending a lot of time together in their big bedroom. Ginger, though, was bewildered, and clung to me.

We decided it would be easier to leave our Riverdale house, with its many reminders of Briggsie, and to start anew. We sold it and moved to a house in Washington, D.C., with more affordable payments. I realized that I must find an additional source of income. Fortunately, Virginia Sargent offered me work doing bookkeeping for her shelter. My two older sons graduated from school and went to work, Jim at the State Department and Bobby at a bank. As a family, we pulled together, and I am so grateful for that.

Peace Plantation Is Born

All through these sad times, of course, we still carried on in our work for animals. In 1948, Alice Morgan Wright, who was — among other things — an heiress, an animal rights activist, an organizer of the United Nations Educational, Scientific, and Cultural Organization (UNESCO), and a sculptress — approached me with an idea.

"Anna, we need to start a national organization," she said, "so we can do the most effective work possible for the animals."

Together, Miss Wright and I started The National Humane Education Society that year. Its guiding principles, reproduced in the following chapter, were authored by Miss Wright, a great lady whose contributions to the well-being of animals are legion.

At about this time, Miss Sargent, who had been running the shelter I worked with, told me she was going to have to close it down. Now I knew I would no longer have a place to house strays and rescued animals. This worried me greatly. I told Miss Wright about the situation, and she promised financial backing to start a shelter under the auspices of our Society.

My son, Jim, and I went out looking for a suitable place. After quite a search, we found a 145-acre place in Sterling, Virginia, with a large house and garage, two sheds and a chicken house. Its price was $50,000. Miss Wright came from Albany to look at it, and offered to donate half the purchase price if we would live on the property. Jim and I decided to take her up on it, and we would meet the monthly payments of this first shelter of The National Humane Education Society.

We sold our house in Washington, receiving about
$6,000 in equity, which we used to put up a frame building
large enough to house about 50 dogs. My sons used their
heads and their hands to do the enormous amount of work
that built our first Peace Plantation, including piping water
from a lake uphill to the kennels, erecting pens, and
painting and concreting.

A Lady Named Ruby:
The Heart and Soul of Peace Plantation

As we prepared for the move to Sterling, I realized how
badly we would need help in caring for the animals. I
turned to my old friend, Ruby Brown, a woman who had
helped me for years by babysitting for my children when
they were little, when I was working or helping at the Be
Kind to Animals Rest Farm. Ruby was a widow with six
children, living at home in an inner- city area of
Washington. Rats were frequent visitors in that
neighborhood, and it was not the best environment in
which to raise children.

I didn't know if Ruby would want to come to Sterling,
Virginia, to be the chief animal caretaker of Peace
Plantation. And in those days, in Virginia, hiring a person
of color for such a responsible post was nearly unheard-of.
But Ruby's color never concerned me. I wanted the
kindest, most loving, most competent person for the most
important job at Peace Plantation. So I asked Ruby, "Would

you like to come live in the country?"

"I sure would," she said. Her curiosity was piqued.

I told her what her duties would be if she accepted my offer to work and live at Peace Plantation: fixing enormous quantities of food for cats and dogs, cleaning their pens and litter boxes, going on emergency rescue missions — whatever it would take to give hundreds of needy animals the best possible care.

It wasn't a job for just anybody, I explained.

"How will I know how to take care of cats and dogs?" Ruby asked me.

"You'll learn," I told her, chuckling. "They'll teach you!"

God was good to me that day. Ruby said "yes," and moved in with us to Peace Plantation on July 1, 1950, its first day of operation. Without Ruby, there is no way we could have handled the quickly growing reputation of Peace Plantation as a great place to take animals in trouble — a place where no healthy animal would ever be euthanized!

My boys converted an open shed into a small house for her, a place she referred to proudly as "my little white house." At first, I could offer her only a very paltry salary, in addition to her room and board. Later, I'm glad to report, The Society was able to pay Ruby more appropriately — but of course no amount of money could ever pay for the kind of love and caring she gave to thousands of animals in her years at Peace Plantation.

Ruby stayed with us in Sterling, then moved again

when we relocated Peace Plantation to Leesburg, Virginia, in 1965. For 34 years, Ruby was the heart and soul of Peace Plantation, my right arm and half of my left. Knowing that Ruby was in charge, I could leave our place to go rescue animals or to raise the money we so desperately needed to keep our operation going. Ruby took to her duties as if she had been doing them all her life, greeting all guests and giving tours to school and civic groups. No animal rescue effort was too strenuous for her. And she loved the animals so much that she would go out of her way to prepare treats for them — stopping on the roadside to pick watercress to add to their meals, making corn on the cob with margarine for the cats, fixing up any little delicacy that might add pleasure to their lives. (Yes, cats like watercress, corn on the cob — and potatoes!)

"I try not to favor any cat or dog in our charge," she would say, "and I strive to pass my love to all of them in my care. No task is too menial when it comes to tending the cats and dogs."

Removing leftover food and cleaning litter boxes never seemed to bother Ruby. Nor did washing the carpets and rugs from the animals' pens — by hand, on a washboard, because Peace Plantation didn't have a washer or a dryer in those days. We all shared in this heavy work. Ruby never complained of it. She felt it was a privilege to take care of the animals.

Ruby's love and dedication showed — in the animals' sparkling-clean cages, in their odor-free quarters, in their healthy coats and eyes, and in their happy demeanor. People from all over the region and even across the country got to know Ruby well when they brought animals to us or adopted them from us.

"Ruby was Peace Plantation," people told me when she died.

That was a terrible day, the day Ruby died.

It was September 8, 1984. I was away from home, in New York City, in the tunnels beneath Grand Central Station. My work there had started in 1972. Two railroad employees had been feeding the wild cats who lived in the station's underground area, but now they were about to retire. They were worried about what would happen to the animals. I went back several times in that first year or so, bringing back many cats to Peace Plantation. Others who helped with the rescue promised to keep an eye out to make sure no more cats remained. They promised to call me if they saw others who needed our help.

I didn't hear from them until 1984, when they asked me to come and rescue many more cats now living there. I put my humane traps out as always, but got only one cat and one kitten. It turned out that some well-meaning ladies, fearing I would nab the cats and have them put to sleep, had fed them already that morning!

Greatly discouraged, I called home to check on matters at Peace Plantation, as I always did when I was traveling. To my horror, I learned that Ruby had been taken ill and sent by ambulance to the hospital.

I got back to Leesburg as fast as I could, but by the time I arrived, Ruby had died of a heart attack. She was 76 years old, one year older than me, and she had been my friend since we met on my 18th birthday. I felt my whole world had come to an end. Of course, the world did not end. No matter how heartbroken we might be, life has a way of going on in spite of our feelings. And we had new challenges to meet.

The area around Peace Plantation was starting to become very fashionable in the early 1960s, as the Washington, D.C., metropolitan area continued to expand into the countryside. My children and I discussed the possible problems of increased taxes and the influx of new families into the area and what we would do if the farms surrounding the Plantation were sold off, subdivided, and developed. Surely people buying fancy new homes would not want to be near a thriving animal shelter like ours. Anticipating changes in the area zoning, we started looking for a new place. We were badly in need of better buildings for our animals; this could best be accomplished with a new place.

At first we asked one of our neighbors if they would sell us 100 acres. This, we figured, would be adequate "insulation" between us and any encroaching suburban community. Certainly, said the neighbor, for $400,000! We laughed. Such a price tag was out of the question! We had been operating on a shoestring for years. For years, I had worked full-time at my Government job, running The

Society and Peace Plantation in the evenings and on weekends. Of course I would have preferred to devote all my time to Peace Plantation, but financial reality would not allow it — just as financial reality made $400,000 an impossibility.

Because property was so expensive in our area, we looked in neighboring states — West Virginia and Pennsylvania. But nothing turned up there, so we kept looking, going into rural New York. At last, we found a 138-acre farm near Walton, a small town in upstate New York. The farm had a small kennel and a very nice barn and stable we could use as temporary quarters for the animals.

In 1983, The Society's Board of Directors approved the purchase of the Walton farm, and endorsed our decision to create the new Peace Plantation Animal Sanctuary there. In May of that year, my daughter's husband, Earl Dungan, gave up his Government job in Washington and went to Walton to get the operation started. So by the time of Ruby's death in September 1984, things were well under way at Walton. It seemed to me that Earl had worked miracles with our new facility, which we moved into late in 1984, taking many trips in our station wagon or pickup truck to transport our animals from Leesburg to Walton.

I only wished that Ruby had been able to share our joy as we dedicated our new facility to the ongoing work of The National Humane Education Society. At first, it didn't feel like Peace Plantation, because Ruby was not there to make it so. But today, in my mind's eye, I can imagine this great lady playing Pied Piper to the hundreds of cats in our much-improved facility in Walton, sharing with them her unbounded love and devotion. And somehow, I think Ruby's spirit is still with us, still blessing our work as only she could do.

Heaven knows we need her still, as the requests to help needy, hurt, frightened animals continue to pour into our offices, and as we strive to meet their needs, doing our best to be one candle in the darkness of a cold, cruel world.

Before I finish telling you the story of my life, I would like to share with you the words of my co-founder, Alice Morgan Wright, because they have become the guiding principles of The Society. Her credo for the way we must think and act towards all the animals on this earth has, in my opinion, never been matched for its clarity, sensitivity, and purpose.

CHAPTER 4:
Our Call to Conscience: Alice Morgan Wright's Humane Principles

In 1963, Miss Alice Morgan Wright, co-founder of The National Humane Education Society, wrote the following article, in which she describes her convictions about the humane treatment of animals. These principles have become the cornerstone of The National Humane Education Society. May they inspire you as they have inspired me over these many years.

— Anna C. Briggs

For many years I have pondered the problem of how I might most effectively continue to help animals and to support humane principles after I am gone from this earth. The fruit of my study and thought is a will bequeathing all that I have to a selected list of humane societies throughout the world and to the Alice Morgan Wright-Edith J. Goode Foundation for Animal Welfare, which will use permanent funds of the Foundation to assist needy humane societies that follow genuine humane principles. For the friends and the humane organizations that are to receive bequests and future grants under my will, and for all friends and defenders of animals, I have tried to assemble a few thoughts and recommendations gleaned from experiences in my long life.

I have become convinced that the worst of all crimes committed are acts of cruelty, and of all the cruelties the most excruciating is that perpetrated by experimenters upon living animals. The recorded tortures of human beings are seldom of such long duration as those inflicted upon some laboratory animals. Some suffer from repeated experiments for months, even for years.

At this very time means are being sought to limit the increase of human population in most parts of the world. Over- population has been called a greater menace to mankind than the atom bomb itself. Yet the justification of vivisection and the torture of animals is alleged by the researchers to be the possibility of finding ways to save human life and to prolong the lives of the very old and helpless.

Cruelty is inflicted also in the name of sport. Each country has its favorite cruel spectacles. Rodeo is billed as that "good, clean, American sport." Cock-fighting is popular. Dog-fighting to the death is enjoyed by some. Rabbit killings by stoning and beating with clubs, in which men, women and children participate, are a traditional festival of a chapter of a well- known organization in our country. We have the coon-on-a-log, the coyote in a pen, to be attacked and killed by dogs for the enjoyment of the spectators.

Since these events are the delight of our public, it is almost impossible to obtain an injunction or a criminal judgment from our courts, although anti-cruelty laws on the books in the states where these events occur forbid the beating of an animal and other abuses.

All of these facts indicate to me that the only hope for the relief of animals is through the long, hard process of educating the human race, from childhood onward, by the teaching of compassion. Let us remember the great gifts of companionship and of beauty which are ours through association with living creatures of Earth and ask ourselves how such sentient flesh could have been thought suitable for sacrifice by torture in experiments endlessly repeated in laboratory after laboratory.

By what right does one sentient being torture another? Does the God of the Christians sanction it? Is it justified even by the hope of prolonging human life in an era when over-population threatens the health and the subsistence of mankind?

In Genesis I, 26 and 28, it is reported that God gave Man "dominion" over the animals. Some modern scholars have asserted that the English word nearer to the original meaning would be responsibility. If in those two verses the Church had read that God gave Man responsibility for the animals, how different would have been the attitude of the Church and the faithful toward animals, and how much easier would be our task of teaching compassion and the prevention of cruelty to animals.

There is one possibility of educating the next generation of the human race in compassion, in our era of speed, through the United Nations' UNESCO and its program of world education. Let us appeal to UNESCO again, and repeatedly, to include humane education in that program. The concepts of compassion common to the utterances of the prophets, the poets, the philosophers of the races of men should be translated into all tongues for all children to understand.

To bring this international teaching of compassion into our own schoolrooms is our duty; to promote insistently in our institutions of learning the education of the heart, and the courage to withstand any popular trend which, in the misused name of Science, might lead to disregard for the fundamental ethics of righteousness and compassion.

In order that this teaching of the school shall also be obtained in the home it is important to urge parents and other guardians of children to take the greatest care in avoiding cruelty and hardship to the animals with which the children are associated.

For putting into practice my thoughts and recommendations I would set down the following reminders — the ways and means:

1. To oppose cruelty in all its forms

2. To strive for an end to bullfighting, rodeo, and all cruel sports wherever performed and wherever represented as art or as entertainment

3. To strive to abolish cruel trapping

4. To discourage hunting, especially as a sport

5. To oppose all poisoning of wildlife

6. To protect and conserve wildlife for its own sake and not as a resource for Man's exploitation

7. To aid or initiate programs for slaughter reform

8. To teach humane handling and care of work animals and food animals

9. To advance programs for the humane sterilization of cats and dogs in order to reduce their over-population

10. To provide for the rescue, housing and feeding of lost, stray or abandoned animals, until suitable homes are found

11. To urge that when it is necessary to put any tame animal to death, unless some better method of euthanasia is available, it be so arranged that the animal be held in the arms of some human friend while it is being given a painless preliminary anaesthetic, to be stroked and comforted with

reassuring words until it loses consciousness,
after which the lethal agent should be quickly
administered

12. To recognize in animals their capacity for
friendship and their need of friends. To befriend
all Earth's creatures, of the land, the sea and the
air; to defend them against ravages by mankind,
and to inspire in human beings compassion for
all

Alice Morgan Wright
Albany, New York
January 1963

CHAPTER 5:
Living the Legacy of Alice Morgan Wright:
PART 1

I n my life, I have found it is never enough simply to think something. You have to be prepared to act on what you believe, or else it's just idle thought-spinning. And while thinking by itself can be a wonderful activity, it cannot change the world. For that, you need action.

That is why I want to give you some specific tips on implementing the twelve principles set forth in the previous chapter. We've come up with 50 tips, one to commemorate each year The Society has been in operation. To me, this is a fitting way to celebrate our half century! You, too, can help us commemorate this landmark event, by putting them into practice in your daily life.

The tips are organized by the way they fall under the broader principles; some of them may not apply to you at all, while others will be very relevant. And, while they are not the only things you can do, I include them here because they represent the cornerstone beliefs of The Society, the ideas that guide our actions each and every day, the practices that can make this world a more humane, caring, and loving place for every animal who is born.

I urge you to study them carefully ... decide for yourself which or how many you can put into practice in your own life ... and talk them over with your friends and family. It is through careful thought, discussion, and deliberate action that we can change the world for the better for the animals. Here are the first twenty-five of them.

I. To Oppose Cruelty In All Its Forms ...
1. Get Involved

If an animal cruelty case comes to your attention, write letters to the prosecutors, judges, and others involved in the legislative process. Ask that those responsible for the cruel act be given strict penalties so that a clear message of abhorrence to cruelty will be sent. Too often, these cases are merely brushed aside by the legal system, and the perpetrators are given only lenient charges. This gives the impression that the animal was worth little, if anything. "Cruelty to animals will be punished to the fullest extent" must be the message that is sent, loud and clear.

Barbarous acts toward animals often lead to brutality to humans; this connection is well-documented. It has been observed that serial killers often began their sprees of violence by practicing on animals. It is unfortunate that many lawmakers and law enforcement officials do not make the connection between the two acts. If they did, we might see stronger laws protecting animals and more real discipline for those who break the law.

We as a society must take these acts of cruelty, however small, very seriously. We need to demand stronger sanctions for crimes against animals. We need to take a stand and proclaim that animal cruelty will not be disregarded. To ignore this violence only invites further violence.

As you write letters to your legislators, don't forget to send letters to the editors of newspapers as well. Encourage friends and family to join in the letter-writing campaign. Even one letter can sometimes make the difference!

I. To Oppose Cruelty In All Its Forms ...
2. Volunteer your time to work with youth.

Boy and Girl Scout troops, church and synagogue youth groups, after-school programs, and summer camps are always in need of extra volunteers and activity ideas. You can create a basic educational program on kindness to animals and offer to share it with these groups. Use whatever medium you feel comfortable with — artwork, puppets, or storytelling are just a few options.

If you decide to take a live animal to your presentation, be sure that both the animal and the children will be safe. Keep dogs on leashes, and make the animal's interaction with the group an organized, positive experience.

Be aware that many animals become quite stressed and overwhelmed when many hands begin reaching for them.

Make it clear beforehand that touching the animal must be kept to a minimum. Lastly, save the introduction of the animal until the very end of your presentation. If there is not an appropriate place to keep the animal during the program, leave the animal at home.

The National Humane Education Society can help you get started! Write or call our office for more information.

I. To Oppose Cruelty In All Its Forms ...
3. Don't accept the argument that vivisection is necessary for biomedical research.

Animals are different anatomically and physiologically from humans, so experimenting on animals in the hope of curing human disease is fallacious. Many respected scientists are now publicly admitting this.

Between 1976 and 1985, the Food and Drug Administration released 198 new medications for humans in the United States. Of these, 102 were recalled or relabelled because of side effects not predicted by animal experimentation. Some of these medications caused blindness, liver failure, kidney failure, seizures, and even death.

Cancer specialists have gone on record in medical journals and scientific publications stating that artificially induced cancers in animals are so different from naturally occurring human cancers that studying animals is meaningless for curing human disease. The prestigious medical journal, The New England Journal of Medicine, published an article by a leading cancer physician, Dr. Bailar, in which he states that the nation's "war on cancer has been a qualified failure." Dr. Bailar advocates prevention as the key to decreasing mortality rates from cancer, not animal experimentation.

Further, animal experimentation has not been successful in pinpointing the causes of heart disease, stroke, diseases of childhood, neurological diseases, psychiatric diseases, and others. However, it is well documented that avoiding a diet of meat and meat by-products, not smoking or drinking, and living a healthy lifestyle can prevent 60-90% of all disease.

Alternatives to vivisection are proving to be more accurate, less costly, and able to provide results faster. Best of all, they are immeasurably more humane.

I. To Oppose Cruelty In All Its Forms ...
4. Do not purchase products from companies that continue to perfom tests on animals.

Animal testing for safety of such products as cosmetics, household cleansers, and chemicals is outdated, misguided, and unnecessary. The Lethal Dose 50 Test, where substances are force-fed into animals until 50% of the test population is dead, and the Draize Test, where live rabbits are forced to endure the pain of chemicals being applied directly to their eyes and skin, are just two of the

outdated tests that are extremely unreliable and very
expensive to conduct. Many companies continue these
tests only to have data on file in case of liability lawsuits.

Today, there are many more responsible,
compassionate companies whose products are available to
consumers. But you must still maintain care and
awareness! Do your own research on companies and their
products, and make sure that the labeling that they are
using is truthful. "No animal by-products" listed on a label
can still mean that the item was tested on animals. The
National Anti-Vivisection Society puts together an annual
book that lists companies and products and tells you who
tests on animals and who does not. You can contact them
for a copy of this valuable guide at:

National Anti-Vivisection Society
53 West Jackson Boulevard
Suite 1552
Chicago, Illinois 60604
(800)888-NAVS (6287)
Fax(312)427-6524
E-mail: navs@navs.org

I.   To Oppose Cruelty In All Its Forms ...
5.   **Don't be too quick to declaw your cat.**

Declawing, which is done under general anesthesia,
involves the removal of an animal's claw, including the nail

and part or all of the last bone of the toe.

There is controversy among humane societies about whether a cat should be declawed. One view is that declawing is unnatural and psychologically harmful, but the other is that it does not involve a hardship and that a cat can learn to get along well without them. Declawing, however, becomes more stressful to the cat as it grows older.

Clawing is a natural form of exercise, and most cats will continue to go through the motions of clawing even if they have been declawed. An alternative to declawing is giving the cat something that can be scratched. Sturdy, commercial furniture works well for many cats.

People good with their hands and imagination can build their own structures using wood, carpeting, burlap, and bark. Owners should also regularly clip their cat's nails, taking care to avoid cutting into the quick or nerve.

II. **To Strive For An End To Bullfighting, Rodeos, And All Cruel Sports Wherever Performed And Wherever Represented As Entertainment ...**

6. **Help international councils and humane groups formed in other countries to eliminate bullfighting.**

Unfortunately, bullfighting is a very popular sport, especially among Spaniards, Mexicans, and other Hispanic nationals. In truth, however, bullfighting is no more of a sport than hunting and other practices where people are allowed to gratify themselves by cruelly mistreating animals for pleasure.

Although some bulls weigh more than a half a ton, they are nevertheless no match for the cunning of matadors and their assistants, the banderilleros. From the outset, the odds are heavily stacked against the bulls, who have been rendered more helpless by handlers applying Vaseline in their eyes and sticking picks and other barbs into the bulls to lower their ability to defend themselves. Six bulls are usually killed during a single bullfight.

Each bullfight begins with the banderilleros attracting the bull's attention and drawing his attack with a red silk work cape; this gives the matador time to judge whether the bull shows a preference to charge with one horn or both. Red is chosen to minimize the sight of blood and other stains. A bugle calls is sounded within ten seconds, and the matador begins his performance. The picadors enter on horses at a second bugle call. When the bull sees a horse, he charges it and the picador must fend off the bull's attack with his pike-pole, planting the point right between the neck and shoulder blades. The horses, too, are frequent victims in the bullfight, vulnerable to horrible disembowelment by the charging bull.

Next, another bugle call is sounded as the banderilleros precisely plant two to four pairs of short, barbed darts in the bull, which make him lose preference for attack with either horn, so that the matador can attack equally from either side. When the time comes for the kill, the matador thrusts his cape forward with one hand, causing the bull to lower his head for the attack. With one hand, the matador sinks the sword into the bull's shoulder blades at the junction of the neck. The blade of the sword should cut through diagonally, severing the aorta and causing almost instant death. If blood appears, it is usually because the lungs were pierced, which is not considered good form.

After the kill, the matador and his assistant circle the arena in victory. While the matador is receiving acclaim, an attendant with a short blade severs the bull's spinal cord at the base of his skull, and the bull's carcass is dragged from the arena. Thus concludes the bullfight — a travesty created not from art or skill but from cruelty and violence.

II. To Strive For An End To Bullfighting, Rodeos, And All Cruel Sports Wherever Performed And Wherever Represented As Entertainment ...

7. Don't attend rodeos.

While rodeos may be fun for some people, they are definitely not fun for the animals. Rodeo proponents would argue that the animals involved are well cared for, in order to ensure the best performance and competition in the arena. However, as amateur and professional rodeos proliferate around the world, the animal care standards lapse and deteriorate.

Animals in rodeos are dragged, tripped, roped, wrestled,

and electrically shocked. Ropes and straps are tied around bulls' and horses' abdomens and/or groin and genital areas.

With this cruelly restraining equipment placed upon them, the animals are then goaded to do things they wouldn't ordinarily do unless aggravated. Electric prods are used to literally shock the poor creatures into a more exciting performance. Poorly trained performers and caretakers can accidentally injure the animals as well as themselves.

Keep these grim realities of rodeo in mind and educate others when the opportunity arises.

II. To Strive For An End To Bullfighting, Rodeos, And All
     Cruel Sports Wherever Performed And Wherever
     Represented As Entertainment ...
8. **Don't attend circuses.**

Since their beginning, circuses have caused animal suffering and, sadly, it continues today. Animals who perform in circuses and traveling shows are supposedly protected under the Animal Welfare Act, but, unfortunately, the laws are not always enforced.

Wild animal acts have always been popular, but the care and treatment of these animals is far from humane, particularly with regard to training techniques and living conditions. In essence, the spirit of dogs, horses, elephants, lions, tigers, and others is broken forever.

It is wrong for animals to be used and abused for

human entertainment. Often, the training methods used on these animals are cruel and can involve whips and electric prods. Animals used in circuses are often made to perform under very stressful, painful conditions. They are also made to do acts that are very unnatural for them. Travel for these creatures only exacerbates their pain, as they are confined in small spaces for long periods of time. Some may never touch green grass under their feet. It has also been discovered that game preserves have purchased retired circus animals for hunting purposes.

II. To Strive For An End To Bullfighting, Rodeos, And All Cruel Sports Wherever Performed And Wherever Represented As Entertainment ...

9. Do not attend greyhound races.

Dog racing is perhaps even more inhumane than rodeos and circuses. The greyhound industry looks upon dogs as merely disposable "things." Thousands and thousands of dogs are produced for the sole purpose of racing. Because the training process for racing is quite difficult, most do not make the cut; these are considered as garbage and are killed.

The greyhound that makes it through the qualifying races and has a full career on the race track can usually count on a life span of about three and a half years. After that, the dog's racing days are considered over, and the owners dispose of the animal by killing, selling, or turning

it over to biomedical research. Rarely is the greyhound
adopted as a pet. Estimates place the number of
greyhounds killed each year at approximately 50,000.
What a tragic waste of life!

II.   **To Strive For An End To Bullfighting, Rodeos, And All
Cruel Sports Wherever Performed And Wherever
Represented As Entertainment ...**

10.   **Be aware of the multiple incidents of animal
cruelty and unethical dealings in zoos across
the country.**

First and foremost, keeping healthy animals in
captivity for our amusement is no way to teach our
children respect for animals and the principles of
conservation. Aside from that, however, abuses have been
documented in all aspects of zoo management, including
the acquiring, housing, and final disposal of animals when
they are no longer fit for display.

Animals are occasionally purchased through wildlife
capture, but primarily through captive breeding programs
in other zoos. Those obtained from the wild are often
gained at the expense of the lives of several other animals
who try to protect their offspring. The death rate of
captured animals in transport is high as well, so that these
practices do more to promote the extinction of certain
species than they do conservation.

Zoo breeding programs are no better sources for

animals, since these programs produce excessive offspring which are often sold off through unethical channels. These programs are sometimes justified as a means of preserving endangered species. Too often, though, they breed animals only to produce "cuties" for baby animal displays, a major tourist attraction. Once these young animals lose their baby appeal, they are disposed of in various ways, as CBS' 60 Minutes has exposed in the past.

Primates typically go to research laboratories as they become harder to obtain by importation from abroad. The hoofed and horned animals, as well as the big cats, go to game farms where wealthy patrons pay thousands of dollars to shoot their "prey" at point-blank range for the trophy to hang on their walls.

Other avenues of disposal include circuses and other entertainment acts, roadside zoos, private ownership by inexperienced novices, and restaurants that offer exotic meats on their menus. These practices are hardly consistent with the zoos' stated aims of preserving and protecting wild animals.

As for housing, zoo exhibits vary widely, ranging from bare cage to simulated natural habitats. Even within any given zoo, the quality of housing is different for animals who are considered display-worthy and those kept out of public viewing pending their disposal. Although an enlarged "natural" setting is certainly preferable to a plain cage, the animal still cannot perform any of its natural behavior. There are no predators, no prey interactions, no

breeding by natural cycles, no migrating or roaming for
forage, and no natural diet.

In short, zoo displays exploit the animals as
entertainment. Little, if anything, is learned from these
exhibits about the importance of animals to their natural
environment or their role in the natural order of life.

II.   To Strive For An End To Bullfighting, Rodeos, And All
      Cruel Sports Wherever Performed And Wherever
      Represented As Entertainment ...
11. **Do not attend fiestas — in the United States or
     in other countries — in which animals are
     routinely abused.**

Fiestas or "Blood Fiestas," which are similar to rodeos
in that animals are subjected to very cruel treatment, are a
shameful event. Typically at many fiestas, chickens are
decapitated, bulls castrated, and goats may be tossed from
church towers to their deaths. Ducks and pigs may be
thrown out of windows down to the street. Innocent
animals are also poked, prodded, and jeered as they are led
to their eventual slaughter. Folk tradition does not validate
this type of cruel event; besides, it has been discovered that
these events were not part of Spain's traditions but, rather,
a recent spinoff organized by the bullfighting industry.
Cruelty is cruelty, no matter the reason, and it should not
be tolerated.

Write to the appropriate legislative heads and ask that

these events be stopped. Also, contact the tourism office in
the area, and politely inform them that you will not be
visiting their city or town until the fiestas are eliminated.

III. To Strive To Abolish Cruel Trapping.

**12. Avoid buying any article made with fur,
including coats, hats, and fur-trimmed gloves.**

The methods used to obtain an animal's fur are
particularly cruel, with the most popular being the steel
jaw.

Most trappers favor using the steel jaw leghold trap
because it is designed to preserve its victims' pelts. The
trap is a spring-powered device with a weight-sensitive pan
and two fixed metal jaws. When a paw or beak comes in
contact with the pan, the jaws snap shut on the body part
with a force equal to a car door slamming shut on a human
hand. For the captured creature, the result is an agony that
can drag on for days.

While a few animals do succeed in chewing off a
trapped limb, this desperate maneuver in turn leads to
infection, starvation, and helplessness. Estimates of the
number of animals taken solely for pelts run as high as five
million per year. These include foxes, coyotes, badgers,
mink, skunks, rabbits, prairie dogs, otters, and squirrels.

Scientific research has demonstrated that animals are
as sensitive to pain as humans, perhaps even more so.
Creatures living in and near water, such as muskrats, may

be the luckiest victims, since they sometimes sink and
drown quickly. Millions of other creatures are captured
unintentionally, since the traps will snare any creature
touching the triggering pan. Even endangered bald-headed
eagles have been snared and left to die in the traps, along
with other eagles, hawks, owls, and vultures.

In short, in the wild, to stumble into any trap is to
enter a torture chamber.

III. To Strive To Abolish Cruel Trapping.
**13. Work locally in your town, city, and state to put
an end to the steel leghold trap.**

Lots of grassroots work must be done in order to ban
the deadly leghold trap. Ask your friends, family, and
coworkers to join you in campaigning against this
torturous device. In 1997, the United States government
upheld a proposal that would allow trappers to continue
using steel-jaw leghold traps for at least another six years.

It will be up to individual states to outlaw leghold
traps. This will only happen with the help of
compassionate people at the grassroots level who are
willing to write letters to legislators and educate them and
others on the excruciating pain caused by these devices.

The European Union has already tried to ban the steel
leghold trap, but the United States in response shamefully
proposed the "six-year" continuum. Voice your disapproval
of this action, along with your requests to ban the leghold

trap once and for all. You will be making a difference in the
lives of millions of animals, who will otherwise be potential
victims of the steel leghold trap.

III.   To Strive To Abolish Cruel Trapping.
**14. Control unwanted rodents humanely by
      adopting preventive methods.**

In addition to being inhumane, lethal trapping and
poisoning only temporarily resolve problems.

The most sound, economical, and humane pest-control
approaches are based upon an integrated strategy that takes
rodent behavior into consideration. Here are a few of the
most important steps to keep those unwelcome visitors at
bay:

   ❧ *Look for signs of rodents indoors, and inspect
        outdoors for possible entry ways. Inspections are
        best done in the spring and in the fall.*

   ❧ *Seal holes with coarse copper mesh or expanding
        foam. Both of these items are available at
        hardware stores.*

   ❧ *Keep areas near your home free of weeds and
        debris.*

   ❧ *Store food in rodent-resistant containers.*

❧ *Put away unused portions of canned and dry pet
food, and throw away spilled food.*

❧ *Check your pantry routinely for torn food boxes.*

❧ *Clean up thoroughly after all food preparations.*

Chances are good that, if you follow these instructions,
you will not have a rodent problem in your home.

IV.   To Discourage Hunting, Especially as Sport...
**15. Don't be fooled into thinking that hunting is
      essential to anyone.**

Hunting is only a short-term solution to complaints of
deer overpopulation. After hunting season, less
competition for food among the surviving population
allows for healthier animals and increased reproduction.
Also, scientific studies have shown that populations of deer
that are annually hunted reproduce at double or triple the
rates of those who are not hunted.

Even killing large numbers of deer does not stop the
surviving deer from eating crops, crossing roads, and
causing accidents. New solutions and designs to this
problem are now working across the country. New Jersey
and other states have recently begun to donate deer
repellents to farmers and homeowners. Minnesota and

Washington have installed roadside reflectors, which have effectively reduced deer-vehicle collisions by more than 87%.

Hunting in residential areas, as well as deep in the forest, can be highly dangerous. Annually, more than 200 people are killed in hunting accidents; another 1500 are injured. Many of those injured are innocent bystanders, not hunters. Companion and farm animals also become unwitting victims each year as hunting season gets underway.

As a society, we need to work to protect and restore key habitats for deer and other species. We need to rally for legislation that will preserve open spaces and provide land for wildlife to inhabit freely and peacefully. At every possible opportunity, speak out for conservation and speak against killing.

IV. To Discourage Hunting, Especially as Sport...
16. Learn the arguments against considering hunting as a sport.

Sport is an activity in which participants are equally matched with their adversaries and provide a true challenge to one another. Hunting does not fall under this rubric.

Records of the past show the ingenuity and inventiveness of the hunters and the materials and technology available to them. Weapons at first ranged from sticks, stones, and specially shaped clubs to sharp, pointed

spears. Next, the bow and arrow became the weapon of
choice, making the hunt somewhat more successful.
Stealth and relentless pursuit played major roles in the kill.
In modern times, however, guns have supplanted most
other methods; guns have dramatically changed the nature
of hunting. Hunting with guns is not a true sport, since
animals are no match for rifles and shotguns.

Today, people no longer need to hunt wild animals for
food. Farmers grow fruit, vegetables, and grains and raise
livestock and poultry for food. Grocery stores prevail in
every community. Americans don't need to eat the flesh of
hunted animals.

Viewing wildlife with cameras and binoculars is a true
sport and is the only form of "shooting" that should be
tolerated.

IV.   To Discourage Hunting, Especially as Sport...
**17. Express your opposition to hunting on public
     lands, and post "No Hunting" signs on your
     land.**

The major argument for hunting by some biologists is
economic: Since the taxes and permit fee hunters pay are
spent on improving habitats, hunters have the right to kill
wild creatures. But this logic misses an important point:
Animals belong to all people, not just the small fraction of
those who hunt. Hunters have no inherent right or special
privilege to kill animals just because they pay special excise

taxes.

As stewards and caretakers of the living things that share the earth with us, we should not act like rulers and tyrants over them. All animals have their own special niche to fill in the wilderness. We properly fill our own niche on earth not by destroying other things but by respecting and enjoying them on nature's terms.

V. To Oppose All Poisoning of Wildlife...
18. Don't use poisons for any purpose.

Following the 1972 Executive Order, the use of three poisons — strychnine, sodium fluoracetate (Compound 1080), and sodium cyanide — was banned on federal lands for predator control. Unfortunately, the bans did not include the manufacture, export, or use of these poisons in rodent control, so they continue to be used to kill rodents. The bans were further weakened in subsequent years.

Poisons have been espoused by those wishing quick methods of killing animals, without considering either the damage to the environment and non-targeted wildlife or the cruelty involved. As an example, Canada Geese have been killed when they ate poisoned oats spread for gopher control, and animals preying on dead or dying rodents have been killed by poisons ingested by the rodents. Furthermore, these same poisons can contaminate groundwater systems.

Poison as a means of taking furbearers or predator

control presents a major threat to non-targeted animals and
domestic pets; therefore, these poisons should be illegal in
all states.

V.   To Oppose All Poisoning of Wildlife...
19. Be prepared to help save poisoned animals!

Keep emergency veterinarian, wildlife rehabilitator, and
poison control telephone numbers handy. If you locate an
animal that has been poisoned, contact one of these
agencies immediately. Calmly list the symptoms and relate
any details that might help in the diagnosis. You must act
quickly in these situations — every second is precious.

After checking to see if there are preliminary steps you
can take to aid the animal, transport it to a veterinary office
or wildlife rehabilitator. Use a cat or dog carrier, dog crate,
or other means of transport to ensure your safety and the
safety of the animal.

VI. To Protect and Conserve Wildlife for its Own Sake
and Not as a Resource for Man's Exploitation...
20. Avoid using inhumane glue traps, and
encourage stores to discontinue their sale.

Glue traps consist of a piece of cardboard, fiberboard, or
plastic that is coated with a sticky adhesive. Sticky traps
are designed specifically for use indoors. Glue trap
manufacturers recommend that the traps be checked "every

24 hours" and that "any mouse or rat still found alive in
them should be killed." The reality of this situation is that
the traps are often left forgotten and unchecked for days.
Live animals found in them are often thrown out with the
trap as garbage, because people are either unable or
unwilling to kill them in a humane manner.

Tests evaluating the effectiveness of these devices have
shown that trapped mice struggle excessively to free
themselves. These poor creatures will pull out their hair,
exposing raw, bleeding skin. They break and even bite off
their own legs in attempts to escape. The sticky glue is
extremely caustic to an animal's eyes. After three to five
hours trapped, the mice defecate and urinate out of severe
fear and stress, thus covering themselves in excreta, which
further stresses the poor creatures. This agonizing torture
can go on for hours and even days.

Please use natural repellents or nonlethal traps if you
have a problem with rodents. Let others know of the
cruelties involved with glue traps.

VI. To Protect and Conserve Wildlife for its Own Sake and Not as a Resource for Man's Exploitation...
21. Step Lightly!

Each time you enjoy the outdoors, think about your
actions. Be very careful when using a campfire. Only use a
campfire where permitted, and be aware of weather and
wind conditions. Before leaving a campsite, properly douse

the flame and sift through the ashes with water and/or a
rake. Make sure that the embers are totally extinguished
before you leave the site.

Don't release helium balloons into the air. Balloons can
be deadly to mammals and fish, who may confuse them for
food. Keep balloons inside; instead of sending balloons off
to celebrate an event, throw bird seed instead!

Don't litter, even with the smallest piece of trash.
Many animals will try to eat people's garbage, which is not
a good thing. Wildlife rehabilitators are constantly engaged
in helping animals who only wanted what they thought
was a special "treat." Skunks and raccoons suffocate and
die when their heads become caught inside yogurt
containers. Soda six-pack rings are infamous for the
thousands of animals they have killed as the rings slowly
strangle the unfortunate victim. Please be responsible and
properly dispose of trash — even if it is not yours!
Remember the wise adage: "Leave only footprints, take
only photographs."

VI.   To Protect and Conserve Wildlife for its Own Sake and Not as a Resource for Man's Exploitation...
22.   Help — don't hinder — wildlife.

If you see a baby bird that has fallen out of its nest, be
aware that the mother bird may be out gathering food. By
just looking and not touching, check the fallen bird out for
a broken wing or other serious injury. If the baby has a few

feathers and is hopping around, he is testing his wings and
trying to learn how to fly; here, it is better to leave him
alone.

If, on the other hand, he does not seem ready to fly and
is not injured, place him back in the nest carefully, using
gloves. If the bird appears injured, place a shoe box over
him to keep him safe, and call a wildlife rehabilitator.
These experts are often able to tell from the description you
give whether or not medical care is required. Do not handle
the bird unless it is considered necessary.

VI.   To Protect and Conserve Wildlife for its Own Sake
      and Not as a Resource for Man's Exploitation...

23.   **Do not buy products made from wood found in
      the rain forest.**

By buying products made from rain forest wood, we
inadvertently support the destruction of more and more of
this limited resource. The rain forests are home to millions
of species of animals and plants. Each tree that is taken
from them is a great loss.

Be aware of the types of tropical wood that are native
to the rain forest, and let store managers who sell these
products know why you chose not to purchase from them.

Tropical woods native to the rain forest:

   ❧ Mahogany

   ❧ Teak

   ❧ Satinwood

❧ Rosewood

VI. To Protect and Conserve Wildlife for its Own Sake
     and Not as a Resource for Man's Exploitation...
24. **Use your buying power to make a difference
     for animals.**

Do not buy any product that is made from the
following:

❧ Ivory
❧ Tortoise shell
❧ Real fur
❧ Real bone (for example, "bone china" is
   exactly what the name implies)
❧ Bear viscera (organs)
❧ Real feathers
❧ Other animal extracts or organs

When you stop buying products made with these
animal items, you help decrease the demand for them on
the market. Once merchants "feel the pinch" and
understand that these objects are no longer popular, they
will stop stocking them in their stores. Likewise,
manufacturers will stop producing these items. You can
truly exert your power as a consumer with this simple step!

VI. To Protect and Conserve Wildlife for its Own Sake
     and Not as a Resource for Man's Exploitation...
**25. Turn your yard, balcony or window ledge into a
     wildlife sanctuary!**

You can feed birds, attract butterflies, or merely supply
wildlife with foliage for shelter. Whatever you do, no
matter how small an effort, you can make a difference for
our wild friends. Bird feeders, baths, and houses, as well as
butterfly and bat shelters are available from many stores.
Since wildlife need water, many people build ponds in their
yards and enjoy the benefits of being able to watch
creatures visit all year round.

Even if you live in an apartment, you can do your part.
A flower box can be made into a bird feeding and watering
station in no time! Use your creativity, always keeping in
mind the safety of wild animals. For example, do not place
feeders and water where companion animals can reach
them.

CHAPTER 6:
Living the Legacy:
PART 2

Here is the second group of twenty-five steps to better care of animals, derived from Alice Morgan Wright's 12 Humane Principles and continued from the previous chapter.

VII. To Aid or Initiate Programs for Slaughter Reform...
26. Avoid buying pet foods containing horsemeat.

Horses processed for meat in this country are rarely treated humanely. The myth of "the glue factory," in which only old, worn-out horses are sent to slaughter, by no means holds true for the contemporary business. A slaughterhouse buyer will put down close to a thousand dollars for a well-bred young horse. This ready cash, combined with the tough economics of keeping a thoroughbred, has lured more than one owner into abuse. Doomed animals include ribbon winners and Kentucky Derby descendants.

The economics of horsemeat demand that animals be shipped quickly in large groups. It is not unusual for buyers to herd up to 50 animals onto double-decker cattle cars, where there is not enough room for the horse to stand upright because of its long neck. Buyers jam animals into trucks regardless of their sex, health, or age. Then, the horses are transported hundreds, sometimes thousands of miles cross-country, in all types of weather. Drivers are not instructed to stop, not even for water. Not surprisingly, some horses fail to survive the trip.

At the slaughterhouse, the horse is stunned with a captive- bolt pistol and then sent down a slaughter chute. Sadly, not all horses are instantly stunned, nor do all make it safely through the chute. The fear these innocent animals experience before death is completely unjustified.

When a horse becomes too old or sick to justify prolonging its life, the only humane option is euthanasia by a veterinarian.

VII.   To Aid or Initiate Programs for Slaughter Reform...
27.   Be a voice for animals who are used for food.

Cattle, pigs, chickens, sheep, turkeys, ducks, and geese deserve your support. Although the United States Department of Agriculture (USDA) provides humane standards for slaughter operations, there are not enough USDA inspectors nationwide to handle the overwhelming job of making sure slaughters are being conducted in the most humane manner possible.

Caring individuals must help out where and when they can. Find out whether ranchers and meat packing houses in your area follow humane measures for raising and slaughtering animals for food. If inhumane conditions are discovered, report them to the USDA and follow up to make sure changes are made.

VIII. To Teach Humane Handling and Care of Work Animals and Food Animals...

28. Be extremely careful when placing a horse up for adoption.

If you own a horse and for whatever reason MUST part with him or her, do an extremely thorough screening of the person or persons who wish to adopt the horse. Slaughterhouses are easy dumping grounds for unwanted animals, and the lure of money — however small the amount may be — can be a powerful enticement for unscrupulous people. Many, many pet horses have died in the slaughterhouse unbeknownst to their former owners. Because there is a heavy demand for horsemeat overseas, the slaughter arena is always available to those who would sell an animal for monetary profit.

VIII. To Teach Humane Handling and Care of Work Animals and Food Animals...

29. Consider eating less meat or becoming a total vegetarian.

Eating less beef is kinder to cows. It also helps save precious areas of the rain forest. Because of cattle grazing, more and more acres of this irreplaceable natural resource are being decimated. It takes much more energy and land to raise cattle than it does to produce grain.

Factory farms raise animals under crowded, stressful conditions and treat the poor creatures more like machines than animals. By reducing the amount of meat you eat, you help to reduce directly the number of animals treated in this cruel manner.

A diet without meat can be a healthy, enjoyable way to eat if you take the time to discover your choices. They are practically limitless! A huge array of vegetarian cookbooks is available to suit any palate, and most restaurants and chefs will accommodate special requests if they do not have anything on the menu that is meatless.

Improved health is one of the wonderful benefits of not eating meat. And consider this — "Mad Cow Disease" will never be cause for alarm for you!

VIII. To Teach Humane Handling and Care of Work Animals and Food Animals...

30. Make others aware of the standard practices of de-beaking and toe-trimming in the poultry industry.

De-beaking is a practice which occurs whenever chickens and turkeys are crowded into warehouses, since the birds are not able to get away from one another and cannot establish normal pecking orders. De-beaking is a

painful procedure which involves cutting or burning
through beak bone, cartilage, and soft tissue. It is not like
trimming nails, as the industry has claimed for years. De-
beaking causes both acute and chronic pain, severe stress,
painful eating, and sometimes death.

In addition to being de-beaked, billions of chickens and
turkeys also have their toes cut off to reduce claw-related
injuries to other birds and bird handlers. Poultry are not
stunned prior to hoisting and shackling on the slaughter
assembly line.

A solution? Reducing the crowding and eliminating
the live hoisting and shackling are certainly better than
having to resort to mutilation.

VIII. To Teach Humane Handling and Care of Work
       Animals and Food Animals...

31. Consider eliminating or minimizing the
    amount of animal products you buy.

With less demand for animal products, fewer animals
will be subjected to needless inhumane suffering.

So many shortcomings in current animal husbandry
can be observed on a typical factory farm. A factory farm,
where meat and dairy producers treat their livestock and
poultry as machines, uses the animals intensively to
produce food without regard to their well-being. Consider
some of these practices of the farm industry:

❧ In USDA-inspected facilities each year, more than 8 billion animals are slaughtered, 7.5 billion of which are broiler chickens, turkeys, and spent laying hens. Added to these are millions of spent breeding fowl and small game birds, birds slaughtered in state-inspected facilities and live poultry markets, and the more than 200 million male chicks destroyed by the U.S. egg industry each year as commercially useless.

❧ When beef cattle are transferred to feed lots, they must share grain on unprotected land with 500-10,000 other animals. At the time of slaughter, cattle are crowded into trucks and are typically pulled, prodded, and dragged out. They are stunned between the eyes with an electric gun, shackled and hung by one leg, and led via conveyor belt past a knife-wielding person who cuts their throats.

❧ Broiler chickens and turkeys at slaughter are hung by their feet on hooks mounted to a conveyor belt, passed over an electric current (which does not stun but immobilizes them), and finally decapitated by a rotary blade.

❧ Of the 2.4 million egg-laying hens in the
   United States, 97.8% are confined in cages in
   which four to nine hens have an average of
   48 square inches each. They are often forced
   to molt prematurely by water and food
   deprivation, and they typically have fragile
   bones from lack of exercise.

❧ Dairy cows are allowed to roam freely much
   less frequently than in previous eras. More
   often today, they are trapped in a concrete
   barn. Nothing interrupts their boredom
   except being milked 3-4 times a day by a
   machine, which continues to milk even
   when the cows' teats are dry.

As you can see, living a meat-free life can mean erasing
certain forms of animal cruelty practiced on a daily basis.

VIII. To Teach Humane Handling and Care of Work
     Animals and Food Animals...
**32. Recognize the fact that humane alternatives
     (such as dyes and microchips) exist for
     identifying food animals.**

Notching, or cutting into an animal's flesh for
identification purposes, is a common practice in both pork
and beef production. In pigs, notching is done in the ear,

and several cuts may be made in one or both ears. Ear notching is extremely painful for the animal and can result in excessive bleeding, infections, and even death.

The most common method of identifying cattle used for beef production is branding. In some states, branding is even required by law to market cattle. Branding is typically done with a hot iron and inflicts a painful, third-degree burn on the animal. Branding is done solely to protect the economic interests of the rancher, as a deterrent to cattle rustling. Cattle ranchers have also devised another identification method, called "waddling," which entails disfiguring the loose skin under an animal's chin so that it is visible from a distance.

Such mutilation of farm animals for the sake of convenience is blatantly cruel.

VIII. To Teach Humane Handling and Care of Work
      Animals and Food Animals...
**33. Help pass an ordinance in your community to
      help downed animals.**

"Downed" means any live animal (including cattle, swine, sheep, goats, and equine species) which is unable to stand and walk without assistance.

The first step is to document the problem of downed animal abuse — at a farm, auction, or slaughterhouse. It is helpful to have pictures and a videotape to show local officials. It is best to provide documentation showing

downed animals in your immediate vicinity. When people,
including government officials, witness downed animal
abuse, they are often moved to action.

Once a proposal has been introduced, it will be
necessary to garner the support of other government
officials. This requires lobbying to convince policy makers
to ban the transport of downed animals.

Remember: Downed animals pose a risk to human
health. Besides potential bacterial or antibiotic residue
problems, some evidence suggests that downed cows in the
United States may harbor a variant of Britain's "Mad Cow
Disease." Most people don't know that downed animals
are used for human food. It can be safely assumed that
they would object to the practice if they were made aware
of it.

IX   To Advance Programs in the Humane Sterilization of
      Cats and Dogs in Order to Reduce Their
      Overpopulation...

**34. Have your pet spayed or neutered to prevent
      unwanted litters of kittens and puppies.**

Female animals are spayed, and males are neutered.
Spaying involves the removal of the ovaries and uterus;
neutering, removal of the testicles.

Spaying/neutering offer distinct advantages over
confinement: (1) The effects are permanent. (2) With the
urge to mate gone, a pet's urge to roam and fight is also

reduced. (3) Blood stains, spraying, and the persistent scratching, barking, and howling to be let out by animals in heat are eliminated. Finally, (4) the threat of breast cancer is reduced and uterine infections eliminated in spayed females.

The cost of the operation will be repaid many times over: Your pet's life span will increase; injuries resulting from fighting over a mate or being hit by a car while in pursuit will not occur; and many local jurisdictions substantially reduce the fee to license spayed/neutered dogs every year.

IX. To Advance Programs in the Humane Sterilization of Cats and Dogs in Order to Reduce Their Overpopulation...

35. Don't be part of the problem.

If you think, "I can let my animal breed, because I can always find good homes for the litter of kittens (or puppies)," you are part of the pet overpopulation crisis. Even if you make it over the difficult hurdle of placing the puppies or kittens, each home that you find is one less home available for the millions of unwanted animals euthanized each year. Spay and neuter all of your pets and encourage others to do the same. Contact The National Humane Education Society for more information.

IX. To Advance Programs in the Humane Sterilization of
     Cats and Dogs in Order to Reduce Their
     Overpopulation...

**36. Don't accept excuses from someone electing
     not to spay or neuter their pet.**

Present him or her the facts:

- ❦ Female dogs and cats do not "miss" the
  feeling of giving birth. The sooner the
  female is spayed, the less she will suffer from
  heat periods.

- ❦ Neutering a male dog or cat does not make
  him fat or lazy. In fact, because your male
  will have less urge to run or fight, he will be a
  better companion.

- ❦ Spaying and neutering are simple, painless
  surgeries performed under anesthesia. The
  operation can actually prevent health
  problems later on.

- ❦ Every litter of puppies and kittens can
  conceivably create thousands of offspring,
  which will likely end up in animal shelters or
  in the hands of uncaring owners.

X.   To Provide for the Rescue, Housing, and Feeding of
     Lost, Stray or Abandoned Animals, Until Suitable
     Homes are Found.

37. Help those in need.

Attend animal emergency seminars and workshops in
your area. Many towns, cities, and states actively promote
emergency/ disaster awareness programs; ask your local
veterinarian for more information specific to pets. United
Animal Nations is an excellent organization that serves
animals in times of disasters; they provide emergency
planning workshops nationwide. You can find out when a
workshop is scheduled in your area by contacting:

United Animal Nations
P.O. Box 188890
5892 A
South Land Park Drive
Sacramento, California 95818
(916)429-2457

In the meantime, talk to your veterinarian and ask him
or her about basic emergency care for your animal(s). It is a
very good thing for a pet owner to know animal CPR
(cardio-pulmonary resuscitation), an animal version of the
Heimlich maneuver, and how to apply pressure to a
wound. Your local library and the Internet are also good
resources for more information.

X.   To Provide for the Rescue, Housing, and Feeding of
     Lost, Stray or Abandoned Animals, Until Suitable
     Homes are Found.
38. Consider keeping your cat indoors.

Traffic, traps, poisoning, and cruel people are just a few
of the dangers that can kill or injure outdoor cats. Disease
and parasites are much easier to avoid when a cat stays
indoors. Cats who are not spayed or neutered and are
allowed to roam will mate and create more cats who will
either die agonizing deaths on the street or be euthanized
because there are not enough homes for them. Outside
dangers are so prevalent that the average lifespan for a free-
roaming cat is just a little more than one year.

Cats are quite content and happy indoors. To help
them adjust, provide them with a scratching post, a few
safe toys, and a window perch, and you have a built-in
kitty playroom! You may want to try growing sprouts of
oats, wheat, rye, parsley, plain grass, or catnip to provide
some greenery for your feline. Nibbling on leaves and grass
helps remove hairballs and aids in the digestive process.
Remember, however, to keep other houseplants out of
reach, since many of these plants may be toxic.

Screened porches make excellent play areas for cats.
Some people even build large, screened enclosures for their
cats, but you needn't go to that extent to make your feline
a happy indoor inhabitant. Contact The National Humane
Education Society for more information!

X.   To Provide for the Rescue, Housing, and Feeding of
     Lost, Stray or Abandoned Animals, Until Suitable
     Homes are Found.

**39. Don't purchase an animal from a pet store or
      breeding kennel.**

The inhumane conditions associated with the
breeding, transportation, and sale of animals in pet stores
are notorious and widespread.

Puppy mills, where female dogs are bred continuously,
are too often lacking in adequate housing, feeding, and
sanitation.

Transportation of pets, which can cover hundreds of
miles by pick-up trucks, tractor trailers, or planes, is largely
unregu lated, and animals can go for many hours without
food, water, or proper ventilation.

Once at the pet stores, retailers are more concerned
with profits than they are with healthy living conditions.
Reports of sick or abused animals are not unusual.

If you have your heart set on a purebred, keep in mind
that animal shelters and humane societies often take in
many purebred animals. If you insist on purchasing from a
breeder, be sure to visit the facility to assure yourself that
the animal was raised in humane surroundings.

X.   To Provide for the Rescue, Housing, and Feeding of
     Lost, Stray or Abandoned Animals, Until Suitable
     Homes are Found.

40. Instead of buying a dog or cat from a pet store, adopt one from an animal shelter or humane society.

Each hour of every day, more than 3,000 dogs and cats are born in the United States. Most of these animals are unwanted and end up in shelters.

Ironically, considering the rampant overpopulation of animals in this country, there are commercial kennels and puppy mills that breed animals exclusively for the pet store market. Pet shops rely on the natural appeal of puppies and kittens, and they know they can sell these animals for high prices. All too often, the new owner leaves the store with no knowledge of how big the animal might get, the type of personality it may have, or any other useful information on integrating this new family member into the home.

For those animals that are not purchased, their fates can be quite precarious. The lucky ones are often taken to overcrowded shelters. The unlucky may end up in animal testing facilities or other cruel places.

The benefits of acquiring a shelter pet are many, including the following:

🐾 You are literally saving one life (and possibly others) when you adopt from an animal shelter. As animals are adopted, this opens up space for other abandoned or stray animals to be taken in and cared for.

❧ The dog or cat you adopt is more than likely already housebroken; even if he or she is not, shelter staff can explain house training methods.

❧ Older cats and dogs have the advantage of known personality and temperament (shelter staff can clue you in!) and size reliability (you already know how big Rover is!).

❧ Adoption staff at shelters work with you to make the perfect match of pet to owner. It always should be made clear that this is a life-long commitment and if, for whatever reason, the adoption does not work out, the animal should be returned to the shelter to

❧ You will be an example to others and may encourage them to look into shelter adoption as well.

❧ There are puppies, kittens, dogs, cats, pure-breds, and mutts in any given shelter, all awaiting new homes. If you are looking for a specific type of animal, most shelters will keep you on a waiting list until they receive that special someone for you!

❖   Many shelters include all necessary shots and
     spay/neuter surgery in the cost of the
     adoption. This is a great way to get started
     with your new friend! Spaying and
     neutering helps to end the tremendous pet
     overpopulation problem and is healthier for
     your pet. This package deal also is less costly
     to your pocket!

X.   **To Provide for the Rescue, Housing, and Feeding of
Lost, Stray or Abandoned Animals, Until Suitable
Homes are Found.**

41. Be prepared!

Always keep a cat carrier, a slip lead (leash), heavy
gloves, an old bath towel or blanket, a can of wet cat food,
dog biscuits, and a listing of area emergency veterinary
locations and telephone numbers in your vehicle. You
never know when you are going to come upon an animal in
distress. These items will help you transport him or her
with the least amount of stress and injury to both you and
the animal.

At home, put together an emergency supply kit just for
your animals. This should include: cans of food, a can
opener, dry kibble food, favorite treats, a bottle of water,
food and water bowls, peroxide, extra collars and
identification of the pets, dog leashes, tweezers, gauze and
sterile pads, Betadine, and photographs of your pets in case

you become separated and need to search for them. Tuck
all of these items away in a canister, and remember to
change the water and dry food every three months. If they
ever become needed, you will be very thankful to have
these provisions on hand.

XI.   When It Is Necessary To Put An Animal To Death, To
      Provide For It A Loving Environment...
**42. If needed and you are able, assist wounded
      wildlife.**

Injured or sick wild animals with no chance of
recovery should be euthanized as humanely as possible.
Veterinarians and wildlife rehabilitators are best suited to
determine when euthanasia is necessary.

XII. To Recognize Animals' Capacity For Friendship And
      Their Need Of Friends...
43. Don't leave a dog chained outside.

Unfortunately, dogs who are constantly kept tied up
outside are many in number. These poor creatures might
be tied to a fence, a porch, or a tree with nothing but a
worn circle of dirt surrounding them. Most of these
"backyard dogs" cannot move far enough to shelter
themselves from the heat or cold. They lack human
companionship, and the question arises, "Why do these
people even have this poor animal?"

Being alone really goes against a dog's basic instincts; as pack animals, dogs need companionship just as much as they need food and water. They want to be with the family, to receive attention from the humans they try to please. Most of these dogs will bark, whine, and claw in their attempts to get close to humans. Some, after enough time goes by, seem to give up and become sad and withdrawn in their behavior.

Under the best of circumstances, a backyard dog is fed and given water daily. But for the many others, semi-forgotten, they are lucky to get fresh water on a weekly basis.

Dogs offer unconditional love when they are allowed to be part of a family. If this isn't what the family has in mind, they truly should rethink dog ownership.

XII. To Recognize Animals' Capacity For Friendship And Their Need Of Friends...
44. Be a responsible caretaker and keep your furry friends safe!

Dogs should always wear a collar with up-to-date license and address information. Whenever your cat goes outside of the house — trips to the vet, stays at a boarding facility, or during a family move — make sure he or she is wearing an identification tag on a breakaway safety collar. Also, double-check to make sure all of the information is correct!

XII. To Recognize Animals' Capacity For Friendship And
Their Need Of Friends...

**45. Beware of the dangers of summer heat and
the hazards of winter weather.**

A dog kept outside during the summer months must
always have a shady, sheltered place to rest, with easy
access to fresh water kept in a tip-proof bowl.

Keep in mind that many dogs are terrified of
thunderstorms and may break out of the most secure
enclosures during a storm. It is for this reason that all dogs
should have proper identification at all times.

Although it may seem obvious to most, it cannot be
overstressed that you should never leave your dog
unattended in direct sunlight or in a closed vehicle.
Heatstroke can occur quite easily and quickly, leading to
brain damage or even death. The first signs of heatstroke
are laborious panting, drooling, and a bright red tongue and
gums. The animal may then collapse.

Should these signs occur, gradually cool the animal
with water, under a cool shower, or give it a cold water
rubdown immediately. However, cooling the body back to
normal is often not sufficient to save the animal's life. So,
you are urged to rush the animal to the veterinarian for
continued treatment.

Likewise, without adequate preparation for the cold
months, an outside dog could both suffer and die.

One of the first steps is to check the dog house itself. The entire structure should be a few inches off the ground to prevent dampness. The outside should be waterproof and draft- free, with an entrance sheltered from wind.

The inside should be just large enough so that the dog can lie down and have a little head room when sitting — but no larger than this, so that the dog's body heat can help keep the house warm. Fresh hay or straw can be put down and changed periodically to provide additional comfort.

Outdoor dogs require extra food during winter months, because the additional calories are used to produce warmth. Of course, clean water should be available at all times and the bowl checked often to make sure the water hasn't frozen.

Most veterinarians do not recommend outside housing for a dog six months or younger; on extremely bitter evenings, it is advisable to bring a dog of any breed inside. Of course, most dogs would prefer the warmth and comfort of your home, even if it's just a little place in the laundry room. Take care to keep your dog away from drafts and provide it with some soft bedding.

XII.   To Recognize Animals' Capacity For Friendship And Their Need Of Friends...
46. Keep your pets up to date on their vaccinations.

Vaccinations are highly effective in preventing

infectious diseases in dogs and cats. Of course, if a pet is already exposed, vaccinating him will not alter the course of the disease. This is why it is so important to begin preventive treatment early on and to keep vaccinations current.

Vaccinations against distemper, infectious hepatitis, and leptospirosis are important for dogs. For cats, the important vaccines are panleukopenia, feline respiratory disease, and feline leukemia.

Rabies vaccines, required by law throughout the United States and Canada, are required for both dogs and cats; without evidence of having obtained a rabies vaccine, a dog license will not be granted.

XII. To Recognize Animals' Capacity For Friendship And Their Need Of Friends...

47. Ask your veterinarian about "wellness testing" for your young or aging pet.

There are two basic kinds of blood tests your veterinarian will typically use for your pet's wellness screen: blood chemistry tests and hematology tests.

Blood chemistry tests provide an inside look at your pet's vital organs. For example, checking chemistries produced by organs like the liver and kidneys helps a veterinarian determine whether these organs are functioning properly.

Hematology tests provide an inside look at the blood

cells themselves. Three reports are common:

1. Red blood cell analysis, monitoring the cells respon sible for carrying oxygen throughout the body;

2. White blood cell analysis, checking on the body's pri mary means of fighting infection; and

3. Platelet analysis, ensuring that the blood can clot sufficiently to stop bleeding when necessary.

Various combinations of these tests help your veterinarian chart your pet's long-term health and wellness.

XII. To Recognize Animals' Capacity For Friendship And Their Need Of Friends...

48. The more time and attention you give, the more you get back.

Sincere caring requires that we take the time for genuine companionship — at least a few minutes, each day, of the best attention we can give. Take into consideration that convenience for the owner often means hardship for the animals.

Whether we depend on animals for companionship or rely on them for more, the caring we show pets today can be so intense as to effectively change or add years to our lives. Recent evidence shows that a more positive outlook, lowered blood pressure and, in some cases, even remission of serious disease have been brought about by the company of a beloved pet. That has led to the growth of pet visitation programs in nursing homes, prisons, and hospitals — particularly pediatric wards where pets have calmed frightened young patients.

Of course, the beneficial effects of the bond between humans and animals are not only seen in institutions. They are also to be seen among almost everyone who enjoys the companionship of a pet. The positive benefits of the relationship are constant, even if they go unnoticed. For the older individual living alone, a pet provides another life to look after and care about
— a companion, and, in some cases, protection. In a family situation, a pet becomes the children's friend and comrade, as well as an important lesson in responsibility. For young and old, pets offer years of good times and fond memories.

XII. To Recognize Animals' Capacity For Friendship And Their Need Of Friends...
49. It's okay to grieve over the loss of your pet.

Unfortunately, our pets do not have the life spans that we do. This means that, after years of fellowship, happiness, and unquestioned loyalty, they die, either naturally or by euthanasia. While such emotional whiplash is most unwelcome, it can be tempered with time.

Acquiring another pet is one of the best means of dealing with the loss of an old friend. Having a young puppy or kitten around starts the cycle anew. A new relationship buds and grows, and, before long, we remember not the last days of our former pet's life, but the joys we got from it — and are now getting from the new pet. We notice similarities and differences between the two, and the void of losing a pet is filled. We feel whole again.

We should consider ourselves fortunate to be able to offer a warm home to a number of pets, and we should cherish the company of each and every one.

XII. To Recognize Animals' Capacity For Friendship And Their Need Of Friends...

50. Always remember: you are your pet's guardian.

With regard to your guardianship, there are a few technicalities, legal and otherwise, that you need to keep in mind:

🐾 License your dog and your cat if your town calls for it. Lost, unlicensed dogs and cats are often euthanized unless they are wearing a tag.

🐾 Check with your local health department to find out how many dogs or cats you are allowed to keep according to your town's law.

🐾 Consider health insurance. A good reason to

get health insurance is so that you won't be forced to place a dollar value on your companion's health.

❖ Provide for your pet in case of your death. Ensure that your beloved companion animal will be provided for by naming a caretaker in case of your death. If you can't find a friend or relative you can trust, you might ask a charitable organization to adopt your companion animal, or place him in a good home.

Be sure to leave this organization enough money to make your animal comfortable for the rest of his life. Providing for your dog or cat in your will is as simple as including a provision such as "If my cat, Piper, is alive at my death, I leave her and $5,000 for her care to my friend, N.N."

CHAPTER 7:
A Home for the Homeless: Peace Plantation Today

I n my years of working with animals, I've gotten to
know some wonderful people — people like Ruby
Brown, like Alice Morgan Wright, like Virginia Sargent.
And I've depended on these individuals to help get our
enormous job done, just as others depend on us to help
them care for their animals when they are no longer able.

So often we receive calls from elderly or ill people who
find themselves unable to keep their beloved pets any
longer. Heartbroken at the idea that they must give up
their faithful companions, they must also try to protect
them from euthanasia, the animals' certain fate should
they go to the local shelter.

I'll never forget one of these individuals — an elderly
man called John. I heard about John through a lady who
was a friend of mine. She had seen him in the check-out
line of a grocery store in Washington, and noticed that he
was buying nothing but cat food.

"You must have a lot of cats," she remarked to him.

"No, only two," he told her. "I can't afford any more."

My friend offered to help John by giving him some
money. She was worried because he wasn't buying any

food for himself, and she knew that often impoverished pet owners will go hungry rather than deprive their animals of food.

But John refused her offer, confiding that his immediate worry was not cash, but a place to live.

"I'm living in a rooming-house, and the landlady tells me I have to leave my quarters by the first of the month. I can't find a new place where I can take my cats and I just don't know what to do," he said.

My friend called me, arranging for me to come and get John's cats. He called these precious companions Itty and Bitty. The thought of parting from them was breaking his heart. When I met him, he started to cry.

"If I could only have gotten some work, maybe I could have found a home for them," he said. John was at least 80 years old at the time, and none too well, but I thought perhaps there was a chance he could find some gainful employment.

"Well, what do you do?" I asked him.

"I'm an auto mechanic. But I'd do anything. Even if I could find work as a gardener! Do you know anybody who needs a gardener?"

I wanted to laugh. I myself barely knew the difference between a rose and a dandelion, and Peace Plantation was in dire need of somebody to keep the grounds in order. "I do!" I said, and I offered John the job in exchange for room and board for him and his cats.

He was thrilled. John and Itty and Bitty came to our

place in April. By June, the gardens and lawns were
beautiful. I thought I had a gold mine in John! Sadly, he
died the following October. But he never had to be
separated from his beloved animal friends, and, at the very
end of his life, he knew the satisfaction of being useful, of
being wanted, and of being cared for, even if it was only for
a very short time.

John was like many of the animals we take in at Peace
Plantation Animal Sanctuary — not in the best of health,
no longer in the prime of life, overlooked by an uncaring
world. For me, his story is a good example of my
philosophy that all life is precious, that every living being
deserves an opportunity to live out its days in peace. And
that's why I am so happy to have a thriving Peace
Plantation Animal Sanctuary operating in Walton, New
York, and a healthy National Humane Education Society,
working hard to protect animals all across our great nation.

A Day in the Life of Peace Plantation Animal
Sanctuary — New York

If you were to visit Peace Plantation Animal Sanctuary,
you'd drive into the countryside, taking New York State
Route 206 to our facility. You'd see a huge barn amidst the
lush, rolling hills, with several additions built on to
accommodate the 600 cats and 50 dogs in residence at any
given time. When you walked through the barn doors,
you'd be amazed: Though so many animals live in this big

structure, there's not a whiff of animal odor there, because the Peace Plantation staff lovingly keeps every kennel, every square foot of space scrupulously clean.

You'd see the cats in their large, airy enclosures, roaming at will, playing on freestanding treehouses or cuddling in wicker baskets or bunks. You'd see immediately that these animals get a lot of love, whether they are with us for only a few days before being adopted by a suitable owner, or whether they are with us for the rest of their lives.

In no case is a healthy animal ever put to sleep at Peace Plantation Animal Sanctuary!

Nor do we ever want to turn away an animal in need — no matter where, no matter why, no matter what condition the animal may be in. Of course, this sometimes means we have to board animals at well-run public kennels. (Sadly, on occasion we have had to turn away animals when our sanctuary was fully occupied and there was no room at local kennels, either.)

The Peace Plantation daily routine begins at feeding time, 8:00 a.m., when our staff swings into operation. Staff members monitor the animals while they eat. If any animals do not eat, they are scheduled for a check by the veterinary technician, just to make sure they are okay.

Once a week, all the animals with a problem are checked over by our visiting veterinarian. But every day, our veterinary technicians and vet tech assistants are on hand to take care of the animals' routine needs. Each new animal coming into Peace Plantation Animal Sanctuary must be checked carefully, immunized, and neutered or spayed if she or he has not been already. That's a lot of care to be given! And all the healthy residents must be cared for, too: petted and talked to, brushed, played with. Some need their nails trimmed or their ears cleaned.

Meanwhile, the feeding dishes must be washed, the animals' areas cleaned, rugs and blankets laundered, and fresh water provided. And the Peace Plantation administrative staff must make sure we are well stocked with food and veterinary supplies, that our facility remains in good repair, and that we respond to the many, many calls for help we get every day. They work, too, to find good homes for our precious charges, and to encourage the local community to use our spay and neuter clinic. Services there are provided absolutely free of charge, as are all of our Society's services, though of course we do hope for donations.

People sometimes say we should charge for the services we provide, but I disagree. The National Humane Education Society is a true charity. When we start putting price tags on our services, people will stop providing their generous, heartfelt donations. I believe we get more support by not demanding payment. Our policy is best for the poor whose animals need help. And my belief has been borne out by the kindness of so many donors across America. . . people who have never even seen our Peace Plantation Animal Sanctuary!

I've been tempted sometimes, though, to ask for payment for our services — only because our funds sometimes get so low, especially in winter, when the animals need us so much. We scramble to find space for them. Ultimately, we plan to build a new, larger facility at Peace Plantation Animal Sanctuary on the 120-acre site we own, as well as a Peace Plantation Animal Sanctuary — West Virginia, near the Virginia border.

But that's just part of The National Humane Education Society's overall plan. And Peace Plantation is just one part of the work we do.

Meanwhile, Back in Leesburg. . .

While my son-in-law, Earl Dungan, oversees the operation of Peace Plantation Animal Sanctuary, with the assistance of our 24 indispensable and dedicated staff members, our headquarters staff in Leesburg keeps up its own hectic pace.

I still live near Leesburg myself, and I spend most of my time — seven days a week, in fact — working for The Society, as does my daughter, Ginger.

That means I might be in our offices in Leesburg with our hard-working staff. What does my typical day include? Just about anything! I might be writing letters to editors of magazines like Reader's Digest to protest pro-vivisection articles on behalf of The Society's members. I might be driving to another state to pick up a family of cats whose

owner can no longer care for them, since she is dying of
cancer, or forced to enter a nursing home.

I might be out talking to people about issues. I might
be writing an article for our *Quarterly Journal,* which goes to
400,000 people across America, our most important
educational vehicle.

I might be talking to schoolchildren or civic groups
about the importance of responsible pet ownership or other
humane issues. I might be peacefully picketing a research
laboratory with other Society members, asking them to
stop putting animals through needless torture.

Or I might be sitting down with our executive director,
Mr. William Kropp, to figure out how to make up the
difference between our expenses — always growing, just as
the number of animals in need continues to grow — and
our income.

That financial crunch is always a worry, especially
with so many animals in need of our help. But we of The
National Humane Education Society have been blessed by
the support of many kind men and women, especially in
recent years. In fact, in January of 1988, I found myself in
Mr. Kropp's office, stunned by an important realization.

"I can't believe it," I told him. "In the 39 years of The
Society's existence, this is the first time."

Unintentionally, I left poor Mr. Kropp guessing for a
few moments of silence.

"The first time for what?" he asked me.

"Why, here it is, the first of the year," I said slowly,

"and all our bills are paid. That has never happened before!"

I must confess I shed a tear or two that day. All my life I have gone begging to get the money needed to keep our animals alive and well. I have not wanted to do it, but seeing no alternative, I have done it willingly.

Now, because the word has spread about our work, thousands of kind people across America have come to our aid. This has just happened in the last few years, and I am unbelievably grateful.

At last, at the ripe young age of 88, I could stop begging!

Still, our needs are many. Often, urgent calls to Peace Plantation Animal Sanctuary ask us to take in one more homeless dog. . . one more family of kittens that will surely die if we don't take them in. We stretch the budget as thin as we can, and we manage to do what must be done. But I live with the fear that one day we may have to say "no" — that we may no longer be able to help. If our facilities were filled to capacity (as has happened on occasion in the past), we would have to say "no." Just the thought of this possibility deeply saddens all of us here who work together to help animals. If only people would be more responsible and spay or neuter their pets, so we could cut down on the millions of unwanted animals in this country!

When these kinds of worries overtake me, I think of my late husband and his never-ending optimism. I think of Ruby Brown and her tireless love for our animals. And I think to myself, "Not only will we never turn away a needy animal — but we're going to serve more and more animals! We're going to dream big!"

After all, God's creatures need someone to speak for them. Every day, more beautiful animals need our help. We must look to the future on their behalf.

That is why I want to share my big dreams with you.

The Future Of The National Humane Education Society

As I write these words, Peace Plantation Animal Sanctuary has many urgent needs. So when I say we no longer need to beg, I mean only that I am freed from the daily worry that our animals might not be fed. We are still operating on a shoestring, as efficiently as possible. The only volunteers we have are several caring ladies who often visit just to pet the animals.

Right now, the buildings and grounds of Peace Plantation Animal Sanctuary are in need of substantial upkeep. To give you just one example: In the very near future, roofing, storm doors, and linoleum on the floors of the animal living quarters must be replaced to ensure that the animals in our care remain warm and dry through the coldest and dampest months of the year. We also need additional vehicles to transport animals — principally for rescue and adoption.

Also, and perhaps most urgently, we need more

housing for our animals. I'd love not to have to board out any animals, even temporarily, because it costs so much more to do so. And, as the demand for our services grows, I want to be ready to accommodate every animal who needs us. We can only hope to do this if we can build new buildings at our Walton facility, and — my fondest dream — establish another Peace Plantation Animal Sanctuary near our headquarters in Leesburg, Virginia.

Optimistic people say "when it happens," not "if it happens." So I'll phrase my dream this way: When we build our second Peace Plantation Animal Sanctuary near Leesburg, I hope we can also fulfill a very old dream of mine by building a national humane education center. Here, children of all ages (up to 100 years and more!) could come and get to know animals, see exhibits about humane treatment of animals, and learn how to fulfill their responsibilities to God's precious creatures, whether they be hummingbirds or humpback whales.

There is a real, pressing need for such a center, and I have longed to build it for over 40 years. Now it is my hope that we will be able to do so — with help from kind people who love animals.

Speaking for Those Who Cannot Speak for Themselves

Of course, there's another major part of our Society's work: animal advocacy. In this book, you've read about a number of simple, practical things you can do today to make an immediate, real difference in the lives of animals.

The work we do is vital, and we are in a better position to do it now than ever before, because our membership has swollen to over 400,000 men and women across the United States. Now, we can rally our forces and make a difference when pro-animal legislation is before Congress. Now, we can stand up and speak for the animals who cannot speak for themselves. And with our combined voices, we can make a real difference.

For me, this is a continuation of the work Briggsie did in the 1920s, '30s, and '40s, the work he was doing on the day he died. It is the crusade whose success or failure will determine the future of billions of animals — even the future of our planet. For if we, the human race, do not care about animal life, then we do not care about life itself. And we will prove it ultimately by destroying our beautiful planet.

Animal advocacy and our rescue and shelter work is the mission of my life, the work I hope to be engaged in until I die, the work I hope will continue long beyond my lifetime, shepherded by the caring, dedicated people who now help me run The National Humane Education Society. My daughter, Virginia Dungan, has voiced her hope of carrying on the work of her parents. She has served as the Vice President of The National Humane Education Society since 1982.

I'm hopeful that Peace Plantation Animal Sanctuary is

the kind of place today that Briggsie envisioned when he started his Be Kind to Animals Rest Farm in 1920. And I hope, too, that he is proud to see The National Humane Education Society's strong membership rallying in support of the causes he championed. I dare to hope that he is looking down from his Heavenly home and giving us his blessing.

Because I love animals so much, dear reader, I'm bold enough to hope that you, too, will give us your blessing. . . that you will support our Society in all its work by making a donation of any size today. You can rest assured that it will be put to good use immediately. If you can possibly arrange to visit our office in Leesburg, Virginia or our sanctuary at Walton, New York, please do so.

If you'd like to help us help the animals, please send your check, made payable to The National Humane Education Society, to the following address:

The National Humane Education Society
P.O. Box 837
521-A East Market Street
Leesburg, VA 20176
Phone 703-777-8319, Fax: 703-771-4048
email: natlhumane@aol.com

It would be an honor and a privilege to have the opportunity to thank you. . . on behalf of the animals!

☐ **YES,** I want to help save the lives of animals in need — and make sure everyone in America knows about the proper treatment of animals! I'm enclosing a contribution to The National Humane Education Society in the following amount:

☐ $10 ☐ $15* ☐ $25 ☐ $50 ☐ Other: $_____

* With a gift of $15 or more, you become a member of The Society and will receive numerous educational materials (greeting cards, a wall calendar, our Quarterly Journal, and more) during the year.

Name _____

Address _____

City, State, ZIP _____

Phone _____

Please detach this page and mail it with your contribution check (payable to "The National Humane Education Society") to:

The National Humane Education Society
P.O. Box 837
521-A East Market Street
Leesburg, VA 20176

Your contribution is tax-deductible to the full extent of the law. Thank you!